To Hear and Proclaim

Introduction
Lectionary for Mass

With Commentary for Musicians and Priests

by

Ralph A. Keifer

National Association of Pastoral Musicians, Washington, D.C.

ISBN 0-912405-01-5

National Association of Pastoral Musicians
225 Sheridan Street, NW
Washington, D.C. 20011
(202) 723-5800

The National Association of Pastoral Musicians is a membership organization of musicians and clergy dedicated to fostering the art of musical liturgy.

CONTENTS

Introduction To The Lectionary For Mass
PROLOGUE

PART TWO

STRUCTURE OF THE ORDER OF THE READINGS FOR MASS

Commentary: To Hear and Proclaim

Introduction
Lectionary for Mass

THE ROMAN MISSAL

Revised by Decree of the Second Vatican Ecumenical
Council and Published by Authority of Pope Paul VI

LECTIONARY
FOR MASS

English Translation of the Second *Editio Typica* (1981)
prepared by the
International Commission on English in the Liturgy

SACRED CONGREGATION
FOR DIVINE WORSHIP

DECREE

The Constitution on the Sacred Liturgy directed that the
treasures of the Bible be opened up more lavishly so that a richer
share might be provided for the faithful at the table of God's word

and a more representative portion of sacred Scripture be read to the people over a prescribed number of years (article 51). In response to these directives, the Consilium for the Implementation of the Constitution on the Liturgy prepared this Lectionary for Mass and Pope Paul VI approved it in the apostolic constitution *Missale Romanum*, 3 April 1969.

Therefore this Congregation for Divine Worship, on the express directive of the Pope, publishes this Order of Readings for Mass, to be used from 30 November 1969, the first Sunday of Advent. Since this date is the beginning of the liturgical year 1970, the readings used will be from Year B of the Sunday readings and from Week II of the first readings for the weekdays of Ordinary Time.

Since the *editio typica* of the new Order of Readings provides only text references, it is the responsibility of the conferences of bishops to prepare the complete vernacular texts, following the guidelines in the instruction on the translation of liturgical texts (Consilium for the Implementation of the Constitution on the Liturgy, 25 January 1969). Vernacular texts may be taken from Bible translations already canonically approved for individual regions, with the confirmation of the Apostolic See. If newly translated, they should be submitted for confirmation to this Congregation.

Anything to the contrary notwithstanding.

From the Sacred Congregation for Divine Worship, 25 May 1969, Pentecost Sunday.

> Benno Card. Gut
> prefect
>
> A. Bugnini
> secretary

SACRED CONGREGATION FOR THE SACRAMENTS AND DIVINE WORSHIP

DECREE

THE SECOND *EDITIO TYPICA*

The first *editio typica* of the Order of Readings for Mass, printed in 1969, was promulgated on 25 May 1969 on the express directive of Pope Paul VI. In keeping with the Constitution on the Liturgy, the purpose of this Order of Readings was to supply the conferences of bishops with the references for all the biblical readings to be used at Mass in order that lectionaries in the vernacular would be prepared throughout the world.

The first edition did not contain the biblical references for readings belonging to the rites of the sacraments and the other rites that have been published since May 1969. Also, once the Neo-Vulgate edition of the Bible was completed, the apostolic constitution *Scripturarum thesaurus*, 25 April 1979, ruled that thereafter the Neo-Vulgate must be adopted as the received Latin text for liturgical use.

Because the first *editio typica* is no longer available, the time seemed right to prepare a new edition. It differs from the first in the following particulars:

1. The text of the Introduction has been expanded.
2. The Neo-Vulgate edition is the source for the biblical references, in compliance with the apostolic constitution *Scripturarum thesaurus*.
3. The edition incorporates all biblical references from the lectionaries for the rites of sacraments and sacramentals that have been published since the first edition of the Order of Readings for Mass.
4. It also adds the biblical references for readings belonging to some of the Masses for various needs and occasions and for readings belonging to the other Masses that were added in the second *editio typica* of the Roman Missal in 1975.
5. This edition also adds optional readings for the celebrations of the Holy Family, the Baptism of the Lord, the Ascension, and Pentecost. Thus these celebrations will have a fully complete set of biblical texts corresponding to the Lectionary's arrangement of Years A, B, and C for Sundays and the solemnities of the Lord.

Pope John Paul II has by his authority approved this second edition of the Order of Readings for Mass and the Congregation for the Sacraments and Divine Worship now officially publishes it and declares it to be the *editio typica*.

The conferences of bishops are to see to it that future vernacular editions incorporate the changes contained in this second edition.

Anything to the contrary notwithstanding.

From the Sacred Congregation for the Sacraments and Divine Worship, 21 January 1981.

James R. Card. Knox
prefect

Virgilio Noe
adjunct secretary

PROLOGUE

CHAPTER I

GENERAL PRINCIPLES FOR THE LITURGICAL CELEBRATION OF THE WORD OF GOD

1. PRELIMINARIES

a) *Importance of the Word of God in a Liturgical Celebration*

1. Vatican Council II,[1] the teaching of the popes,[2] and various postconciliar documents of the Roman congregations[3] have

---

[1] See especially Vatican Council II, Constitution on the Liturgy, nos. 7, 24, 33, 35, 48, 51, 52, 56; Dogmatic Constitution on Divine Revelation, nos. 1, 21, 25, 26; Decree on the Missionary Activity of the Church, no. 6; Decree on the Ministry and Life of Priests, no. 18.

[2] Among the spoken or written papal statements, see espcially: Paul VI, motu proprio *Ministeria quaedam*, 15 Aug. 1972, no. V: AAS 64 (1972) 532; apostolic exhortation *Marialis cultus*, 2 Feb. 1974, no. 12: AAS 66 (1974) 125–126; apostolic exhortation *Evangelii nuntiandi*, 8 Dec. 1975, nos. 28, 43, 47: AAS 68 (1976) 24–25, 33–34, 36–37. John Paul II, apostolic constitution *Scripturarum thesaurus*, 25 April 1979: in *Nova Vulgata Bibliorum Sacrorum* (Vatican Polyglot Press, 1979) V-VIII; apostolic exhortation *Catechesi tradendae*, 16 Oct. 1979, nos. 23, 27, and 48: AAS 71 (1979) 1296–1297, 1298–1299 and 1316; epistle *Dominicae Cenae*, 24 Feb. 1980, no. 10: AAS 72 (1980) 134–137.

[3] See, for example, Congregation of Rites, instruction *Eucharisticum Mysterium*, 25 May 1967, no. 10: AAS 59 (1967) 547–548. Congregation for Divine Worship, instruction *Liturgicae instaurationes*, 5 Sept. 1970, no. 2: AAS 62 (1970) 695–696. Congregation for the Clergy, *Directorium catechisticum generale*, 11 April 1971, nos. 10–12 and 25: AAS 64 (1972) 106–107 and 114. Congregation for Divine Worship, General Instruction of the Roman Missal, nos. 9, 11, 24, 33, 60, 62 316, 320. Congregation for Catholic Education, instruction on liturgical formation in seminaries *In ecclesiasticam*, 3 June 1979, nos. 11, 52, and Appendix, no. 15. Congregation for the Sacraments and Divine Worship, instruction *Inaestimabile Donum*, 3 April 1980, nos. 1, 2, 3: AAS 72 (1980) 333–334.

already made many excellent statements about the importance of the word of God and about reestablishing the use of Scripture in every celebration of the liturgy. The Introduction of the 1969 edition of the Order of Readings for Mass has clearly stated and briefly explained some of the more important principles.[4]

On the occasion of this new edition of the Order of Readings for Mass, requests have come from many quarters for a more detailed exposition of the same principles. In response, this expanded and more helpful arrangement of the Introduction first gives a general statement on the close relationship between the word of God and the liturgical celebration,[5] then deals in greater detail with the word of God in the celebration of Mass, and, finally, explains the precise structure of the Order of Readings for Mass.

b) Terms Used to Refer to the Word of God

2. For the sake of clear and precise language on this topic, a definition of terms might well be expected as a prerequisite. Nevertheless this Introduction will simply use the same terms employed in conciliar and postconciliar documents. Furthermore it will use "sacred Scripture" and "word of God" interchangeably throughout when referring to the books written under the inspiration of the Holy Spirit, thus avoiding any confusion of language or meaning.[6]

c) Significance of the Word of God in the Liturgy

3. The many riches contained in the word of God are admirably brought out in the different kinds of liturgical celebrations and liturgical assemblies. This takes place as the unfolding mystery of Christ is recalled during the course of the liturgical year, as the Church's sacraments and sacramentals are celebrated, or as the faithful respond individually to the Holy Spirit working within

---

[4] See *The Roman Missal* revised by decree of the Second Vatican Ecumenical Council, published by authority of Pope Paul VI [hereafter, *The Roman Missal*], *Lectionary for Mass* (1969; Eng. tr. 1969), Introduction, nos. 1–7; decree of promulgation: AAS 61 (1969) 548–549.

[5] See Vatican Council II, Constitution on the Liturgy, nos. 35, 56. Paul VI, apostolic exhortation *Evangelii nuntiandi*, 8 Dec. 1975, nos. 28, 47: AAS 68 (1976) 24–25, 36–37. John Paul II, epistle *Dominicae Cenae*, 24 Feb. 1980, nos. 10, 11, 12: AAS 72 (1980) 134–146.

[6] For example, the terms, *word of God, sacred Scripture, Old and New Testament, reading(s) of the word of God, reading(s) from sacred Scripture, celebration(s) of the word of God,* etc.

them.[7] For then the liturgical celebration, based primarily on the word of God and sustained by it, becomes a new event and enriches the word itself with new meaning and power. Thus in the liturgy the Church faithfully adheres to the way Christ himself read and explained the Scriptures, beginning with the "today" of his coming forward in the synagogue and urging all to search the Scriptures.[8]

2. LITURGICAL CELEBRATION OF THE WORD OF GOD

a) *Proper Character of the Word of God in the Liturgical Celebration*

4. In the celebration of the liturgy the word of God is not voiced in only one way[9] nor does it always stir the hearts of the hearers with the same power. Always, however, Christ is present in his word;[10] as he carries out the mystery of salvation, he sanctifies us and offers the Father perfect worship.[11]

Moreover, the word of God unceasingly calls to mind and extends the plan of salvation, which achieves its fullest expression in the liturgy. The liturgical celebration becomes therefore the continuing, complete, and effective presentation of God's word.

That word constantly proclaimed in the liturgy is always, then, a living, active word[12] through the power of the Holy Spirit. It expresses the Father's love that never fails in its effectiveness toward us.

---

[7] Thus the same text may be read or used for diverse reasons on diverse occasions and celebrations of the liturgical year; this has to be remembered in the homily, pastoral exegesis, and catechesis. The indexes of this volume will show, for example, that Romans 6 or 8 is used in various liturgical seasons and celebrations of the sacraments and sacramentals.

[8] See Luke 4:16–21, 24:25–35 and 44–49.

[9] In the celebration of Mass, for example, there is *proclamation, reading,* etc. (see General Instruction of the Roman Missal, nos. 21, 23, 95, 131, 146, 234, 235). There are also other celebrations of the word of God in the Roman Pontifical, Ritual, and Liturgy of the Hours, as revised by decree of Vatican Council II.

[10] See Vatican Council II, Constitution on the Liturgy, nos. 7, 33. Mark 16:19–20; Matthew 28:20. St. Augustine, *Sermo* 85, 1: "The Gospel is the mouth of Christ. He is seated at the right hand of the Father, yet continues to speak on earth" (PL 37:520; see also *In Io. Ev. tract,* 30, 1: PL 35, 1632; CCL 36, 289). *Pontificale Romano-Germanicum:* "As the gospel is read Christ speaks with his own mouth to the people . . .; the gospel resounds in the church as though Christ himself were speaking to them" (See C. Vogel and R. Elze, eds., *Le Pontifical Romano-germanique du dixieme siecle. Le Texte I,* Vatican City, 1963/XCIV, 18, 334); *idem:* "At the moment Christ approaches, that is at the gospel of the Mass, we put aside our staffs, because we have no need of human assistance" (ibid. XCIV, 23, 335).

[11] See Vatican Council II, Constitution on the Liturgy, no. 7.

[12] See Hebrews 4:12.

b) The Word of God in the Plan of Salvation

5. When in celebrating the liturgy the Church proclaims both the Old and New Testament, it is proclaiming one and the same mystery of Christ.

The New Testament lies hidden in the Old; the Old Testament comes fully to light in the New.[13] Christ himself is the center and fullness of all Scripture, as he is of the entire liturgy.[14] Thus the Scriptures are the living waters from which all who seek life and salvation must drink.

The more profound our understanding of the liturgical celebration, the higher our appreciation of the importance of God's word. Whatever we say of the one, we can in turn say of the other, because each recalls the mystery of Christ and each in its own way causes that mystery to be ever present.

c) The Word of God in the Liturgical Participation of the Faithful

6. In celebrating the liturgy, the Church faithfully echoes the Amen that Christ, the mediator between God and humanity, uttered once for all as he shed his blood to seal God's new covenant in the Holy Spirit.[15]

When God shares his word with us, he awaits our response, that is, our listening and our adoring "in Spirit and in truth" (John 4:23). The Holy Spirit makes our response effective, so that what we hear in the celebration of the liturgy we carry out in the way we live: "Be doers of the word and not hearers only" (James 1:22).

The liturgical celebration and the faithful's participation receive outward expression in actions, gestures, and words. These derive their full meaning not simply from their origin in human experience but from the word of God and the economy of salvation, their point of reference. Accordingly, the faithful's participation in the liturgy increases to the degree that as they listen to the word of God spoken in the liturgy they strive harder to commit themselves to the Word of God made flesh in Christ. They endeavor to

---

[13] See St. Augustine, *Quaestionum in Heptateuchum liber* 2, 73: PL 34, 623; CCL 33, 106. Vatican Council II, Dogmatic Constitution on Divine Revelation, no. 16.

[14] See St. Jerome: "If, as St. Paul says (1 Corinthians 1:24), Christ is the power of God and the wisdom of God, anyone who does not know the Scriptures does not know the power of God or his wisdom. For not to know the Scriptures is not to know Christ" (*Commentarii in Isaiam prophetam. Prologus*: PL 24, 17A; CCL 73, 1). Vatican Council II, Dogmatic Constitution on Divine Revelation, no. 25.

[15] See 2 Corinthians 1:20–22.

conform their way of life to what they celebrate in the liturgy, and then in turn to bring to the celebration of the liturgy all that they do in life.[16]

3. THE WORD OF GOD IN THE LIFE OF THE "PEOPLE OF THE COVENANT"

a) The Word of God in the Church's Life

7. In the hearing of God's word the Church is built up and grows, and in the signs of the liturgical celebration God's many wonderful, past works in the history of salvation are symbolically presented anew. God in turn makes use of the assembly of the faithful who celebrate the liturgy in order that his word may speed on in triumph and his name be exalted among all peoples.[17]

Whenever, therefore, the Church, gathered by the Holy Spirit for liturgical celebration,[18] announces and proclaims the word of God, it has the experience of being a new people in whom the covenant made in the past is fulfilled. Baptism and confirmation in the Spirit have made all the faithful messengers of God's word because of the grace of hearing they have received. They must therefore be the bearers of the same word in the Church and in the world, at least by the witness of their way of life.

The word of God proclaimed in the celebration of his mysteries does not address present conditions alone but looks back to past events and forward to what is yet to come. Thus God's word shows us what we should hope for with such a longing that in this changing world our hearts will be set on the place of our true joy.[19]

b) How the Word of God is Proposed in the Church

8. By Christ's own will there is an ordered diversity of members in the new people of God and each has different duties and responsibilities toward the word of God. Accordingly, the faithful listen to God's word and dwell on its meaning, but only those expound the word of God who have the office of teaching by virtue of ordination or who have been entrusted with exercising that ministry.

This is how in teaching, life, and worship the Church keeps alive and passes on to every generation all that it is, all that it believes.

---

[16] See Vatican Council II, Constitution on the Liturgy, no. 10.

[17] See 2 Thessalonians 3:1

[18] See *The Roman Missal*, opening prayers A, B, and C in the Mass for the Universal Church. St. Cyprian, *De oratione dominica* 23:PL 4, 553; CSEL 3/2, 285; CCL 3A, 105. St. Augustine, *Sermo* 71, 20, 33: PL 38, 463ff.

[19] See *The Roman Missal*, opening prayer for the Twenty-First Sunday in Ordinary Time.

Thus with the passage of the centuries, the Church is ever to advance toward the fullness of divine truth until God's word is wholly accomplished in it.[20]

c) Connection Between the Word of God Proclaimed and the Working of the Holy Spirit

9. The working of the Holy Spirit is needed if the word of God is to make what we hear outwardly have its effect inwardly. Because of the Holy Spirit's inspiration and support, the word of God becomes the foundation of the liturgical celebration and the rule and support of all our life.

The working of the Holy Spirit precedes, accompanies, and brings to completion the whole celebration of the liturgy. But the Spirit also brings home[21] to each person individually everything that in the proclamation of the word of God is spoken for the good of the whole assembly of the faithful. In strengthening the unity of all, the Holy Spirit at the same time fosters a diversity of gifts and furthers their multiform operation.

d) Close Relationship Between the Word of God and the Mystery of the Eucharist

10. The Church has honored the word of God and the eucharistic mystery with the same reverence, although not with the same worship, and has always and everywhere intended and endorsed such honor. Moved by the example of its Founder, the Church has never ceased to celebrate his paschal mystery by coming together to read "in all the Scriptures the things written about him" (Luke 24:27) and to carry out the work of salvation through the celebration of the memorial of the Lord and through the sacraments. "The preaching of the word is necessary for the sacramental ministry. For the sacraments are sacraments of faith and faith has its origin and sustenance in the word."[22]

The Church is nourished spiritually at the table of God's word and at the table of the eucharist:[23] from the one it grows in wisdom and from the other in holiness. In the word of God the divine covenant is announced; in the eucharist the new and everlasting cove-

---

[20] See Vatican Council II, Dogmatic Constitution on Divine Revelation, no. 8.

[21] See John 14:15–17, 25#16; 15:26–16:15.

[22] See Vatican Council II, Decree on the Ministry and Life of Priests, no. 4.

[23] See Vatican Council II, Constitution on the Liturgy, no. 51; Decree on the Ministry and Life of Priests, no. 18; also Dogmatic Constitution on Divine Revelation, no. 21; Decree on the Missionary Activity of the Church, no. 6. See General Instruction of the Roman Missal, no. 8.

nant is renewed.The spoken word of God brings to mind the history of salvation; the eucharist embodies it in the sacramental signs of the liturgy.

It can never be forgotten, therefore, that the divine word read and proclaimed by the Church in the liturgy has as its one goal the sacrifice of the New Covenant and the banquet of grace, that is, the eucharist. The celebration of Mass in which the word is heard and the eucharist is offered and received forms but one single act of divine worship.[24] That act offers the sacrifice of praise to God and makes available to God's creatures the fullness of redemption.

---

[24] Vatican Council II, Constitution on the Liturgy, no. 56.

PART ONE
THE WORD OF GOD IN THE CELEBRATION OF MASS

CHAPTER II

CELEBRATION OF THE LITURGY OF THE WORD AT MASS

1. ELEMENTS OF THE LITURGY OF THE WORD AND THEIR RITES

11. "Readings from Scripture and the chants between the readings form the main part of the liturgy of the word. The homily, profession of faith, and general intercessions or prayer of the faithful expand and complete this part of the Mass."[25]

a) Biblical Readings

12. In the celebration of Mass the biblical readings with their accompanying scriptural chants may not be omitted, shortened, or, worse still, replaced by nonbiblical readings.[26] For it is from the word of God handed down in writing that even now "God is

---

[25] General Instruction of the Roman Missal, no. 33.

[26] See Congregation for Divine Worship, instruction *Liturgicae instaurationes*, 5 Sept. 1970, no. 2: AAS 62 (1970) 695–696. John Paul II, epistle *Dominicae Cenae*, 24 Feb. 1980, no. 10: AAS 72 (1980) 134–137. Congregation for the Sacraments and Divine Worship, instruction *Inaestimabile Donum*, 3 April 1980, no. 1: AAS 72 (1980) 333.

speaking to his people"[27] and it is from the continued use of Scripture that the people of God, docile to the Holy Spirit under the light of faith, receive the power to be Christ's living witnesses before the world.

13. The reading of the gospel is the high point of the liturgy of the word. For this the other readings, in their established sequence from the Old to the New Testament, prepare the assembly.

14. A speaking style on the part of the readers that is audible, clear, and intelligent is the first means of transmitting the word of God properly to the assembly. The readings, taken from the approved editions,[28] may be sung in a way suited to different languages. This singing, however, must serve to stress the words, not obscure them. On occasions when the readings are in Latin, they are to be sung to the melody given in the *Ordo cantus Missae.*[29]

15. There may be concise introductions before the readings, especially the first. The style proper to such comments must be respected, that is, they must be simple, faithful to the text, brief, well prepared, and properly varied to suit the text they introduce.[30]

16. In a Mass with a congregation the readings are always to be proclaimed at the lectern.[31]

17. Of all the rites connected with the liturgy of the word, the reverence due to the gospel reading must receive special attention.[32] Where there is a Book of the Gospels that has been carried in by the deacon or reader during the entrance procession,[33] it is most fitting that the deacon or a priest, when there is no deacon, take the book from the altar[34] and carry it to the lectern. He is preceded by servers with candles and incense or other symbols of reverence that may be customary. As the faithful stand and acclaim the Lord, they show honor to the Book of the Gospels. The deacon who is to read the gospel, bowing in front of the one presiding, asks and receives the blessing. When no deacon is pre-

---

[27] Constitution on the Liturgy, no. 33.

[28] See no. 111 of this Introduction.

[29] See *Missale Romanum ex Decreto Sacrosancti Oecumenici Concilii Vaticani II instauratum, auctoritate Pauli Pp. VI promulgatum, Ordo cantus Missae* (ed. typ., 1972), *Praenotanda,* nos. 4, 6, 10.

[30] See General Instruction of the Roman Missal, no. 11.

[31] See ibid., no. 272 and nos. 32–34 of this Introduction.

[32] See General Instruction of the Roman Missal, nos. 35, 95.

[33] See ibid., nos. 82–84.

[34] See ibid., nos. 94, 131.

sent, the priest, bowing before the altar, prays quietly: *Almighty God, cleanse my heart. . .* [35]

At the lectern the one who proclaims the gospel greets the people, who are standing, and announces the reading as he makes the sign of the cross on forehead, mouth, and breast. If incense is used, he next incenses the book, then reads the gospel. When finished, he kisses the book, saying the appointed words quietly.

Even if the gospel itself is not sung, it is appropriate for *The Lord be with you, A reading from the holy gospel. . .*, and at the end *This is the Gospel of the Lord* to be sung, in order that the assembly may also sing its acclamations. This is a way both of bringing out the importance of the gospel reading and of stirring up the faith of those who hear it.

18. At the conclusion of the other readings, *This is the word of the Lord* may be sung, even by someone other than the reader; all respond with the acclamation. In this way the gathered assembly pays reverence to the word of God it has listened to in faith and gratitude.

b) Responsorial Psalm

19. The responsorial psalm, also called the gradual, has great liturgical and pastoral significance because it is "an integral part of the liturgy of the word." [36] Accordingly, the people must be continually instructed on the way to perceive the word of God speaking in the psalms and to turn these psalms into the prayer of the Church. This, of course, "will be achieved more readily if a deeper understanding of the psalms, in the meaning in which they are used in the liturgy, is more diligently promoted among the clergy and communicated to all the faithful by means of appropriate catechesis." [37]

A brief remark may be helpful about the choice of the psalm and response as well as their correspondence to the readings.

20. As a rule the responsorial psalm should be sung. There are two established ways of singing the psalm after the first reading:

[35] See *The Roman Missal*, Order of Mass, "Liturgy of the Word: The Gospel."

[36] General Instruction of the Roman Missal, no. 36.

[37] Paul VI, apostolic constitution *Laudis canticum* in *The Liturgy of the Hours* [*The Divine Office*] revised by decree of the Second Vatican Council and published by authority of Pope Paul VI (1971; Eng. tr. 1974). See also Constitution on the Liturgy, nos. 24, 90. Congregation of Rites, instruction on music in the liturgy, *Musicam Sacram*, 5 March 1967, no. 39: AAS 59 (1967) 311. General Instruction of the Liturgy of the Hours, nos. 23 and 109. Congregation for Catholic Education, *Ratio fundamentalis* [Basic Plan for Priestly Formation], no. 53.

responsorially and directly. In responsorial singing, which, as far as possible, is to be given preference, the psalmist or cantor of the psalm sings the psalm verse and the whole congregation joins in by singing the response. In direct singing of the psalm there is no intervening response by the community; either the psalmist or cantor of the psalm sings the psalm alone as the community listens or else all sing it together.

21. The singing of the psalm, or even of the response alone, is a great help toward understanding and meditating on the psalm's spiritual meaning.

To foster the congregation's singing, every means available in the various cultures is to be employed. In particular use is to be made of all the relevant options provided in the Order of Readings for Mass[38] regarding responses corresponding to the different liturgical seasons.

22. When not sung, the psalm after the reading is to be recited in a manner conducive to meditation on the word of God.[39]

The responsorial psalm is sung or recited by the psalmist or cantor at the lectern.[40]

c) *Acclamation Before the Reading of the Gospel*

23. The *Alleluia* or, as the liturgical season requires, the verse before the gospel, is also a "rite or act standing by itself."[41] It serves as the assembled faithful's greeting of welcome to the Lord who is about to speak to them and as an expression of their faith through song.

The *Alleluia* or the verse before the gospel must be sung and during it all stand. It is not to be sung only by the cantor who intones it or by the choir, but by the whole congregation together.[42]

d) *Homily*

24. Through the course of the liturgical year the homily sets forth the mysteries of faith and the standards of the Christian life on the basis of the sacred text. Beginning with the Constitution on the

---

[38] See nos. 89–90 of this Introduction.

[39] See General Instruction of the Roman Missal, nos. 18 and 39.

[40] See ibid., no. 272 and nos. 32ff. of this Introduction.

[41] See General Instruction of the Roman Missal, no. 39.

[42] See also ibid., nos. 37–39. *Missale Romanum ex Decreto Sacrosancti Concilii Oecumenici Vaticani II instauratum, auctoritate Pauli Pp. VI promulgatum Ordo cantus Missae, Praenotanda*, nos. 7–9; *Graduale Romanum* (1974), *Praenotanda*, no. 7; *Graduale simplex* (2nd ed. typ., 1975), *Praenotanda*, no. 16.

Liturgy, the homily as part of the liturgy of the word[43] has been repeatedly and strongly recommended and in some cases it is obligatory. As a rule it is to be given by the one presiding.[44] The purpose of the homily at Mass is that the spoken word of God and the liturgy of the eucharist may together become "a proclamation of God's wonderful works in the history of salvation, the mystery of Christ."[45] Through the readings and homily Christ's paschal mystery is proclaimed; through the sacrifice of the Mass it becomes present.[46] Moreover Christ himself is also always present and active in the preaching of his Church.[47]

Whether the homily explains the biblical word of God proclaimed in the readings or some other text of the liturgy,[48] it must always lead the community of the faithful to celebrate the eucharist wholeheartedly, "so that they may hold fast in their lives to what they have grasped by their faith."[49] From this living explanation, the word of God proclaimed in the readings and the Church's celebration of the day's liturgy will have greater impact. But this demands that the homily be truly the fruit of meditation, carefully prepared, neither too long nor too short, and suited to all those present, even children and the uneducated.[50]

At a concelebration, the celebrant or one of the concelebrants as a rule gives the homily.[51]

25. On the prescribed days, that is, Sundays and holydays of obligation, there must be a homily in all Mases celebrated with a congregation, even Masses on the preceding evening.[52] There is also to

---

[43] See Constitution on the Liturgy, no. 52. Congregation of Rites, instruction *Inter Oecumenici*, 26 Sept. 1964, no. 54: AAS 56 (1964) 890.

[44] See General Instruction of the Roman Missal, no. 42.

[45] See Constitution on the Liturgy, no. 35, 2.

[46] See ibid., nos. 6 and 47.

[47] See Paul VI, encyclical *Mysterium Fidei*, 3 Sept. 1965: AAS 57 (1965) 753. Vatican Council II, Decree on the Missionary Activity of the Church, no. 9. Paul VI, apostolic exhortation *Evangelii nuntiandi*, 8 Dec. 1975, no. 43: AAS 69 (1976) 33–34.

[48] See Vatican Council II, Constitution on the Liturgy, no. 35, 2. General Instruction of the Roman Missal, no. 41.

[49] Vatican Council II, Constitution on the Liturgy, no. 10.

[50] See John Paul II, apostolic exhortation *Catechesi tradendae*, 16 Oct. 1979, no. 48: AAS 71 (1979) 1316.

[51] See General Instruction of the Roman Missal, no. 165.

[52] See ibid., no. 42. See also Congregation of Rites, instruction *Eucharisticum Mysterium*, 25 May 1967, no. 28: AAS 59 (1967) 556–557.

be a homily in Masses with children and with special groups.[53]

A homily is strongly recommended on the weekdays of Advent, Lent, and the Easter season for the sake of the faithful who regularly take part in the celebration of Mass; also on other feasts and occasions when a large congregation is present.[54]

26. The priest celebrant gives the homily either at the chair, standing or sitting, or at the lectern.[55]

27. Any necessary announcements are to be kept completely separate from the homily; they must take place following the prayer after communion.[56]

e) Silence

28. The liturgy of the word must be celebrated in a way that fosters meditation; clearly, any sort of haste that hinders reflectiveness must be avoided. The dialogue between God and his people taking place through the Holy Spirit demands short intervals of silence, suited to the assembly, as an opportunity to take the word of God to heart and to prepare a response to it in prayer.

Proper times for silence during the liturgy of the word are, for example, before this liturgy begins, after the first and the second reading, after the homily.[57]

f) Profession of Faith

29. The symbol or profession of faith, said when the rubrics require, has as its purpose in the celebration of Mass that the gathered faithful may respond and give assent to the word of God heard in the readings and through the homily, and that before they begin to celebrate in the eucharist the mystery of faith they may call to mind the rule of faith in a formulary approved by the Church.[58]

g) General Intercessions or Prayer of the Faithful

30. Enlightened by God's word and in a sense responding to it, the

---

[53] See Congregation for Divine Worship, instruction *Actio pastoralis*, 15 May 1969, no. 6g: AAS 61 (1969) 809; *Directory for Masses with Children* (1973; Eng. tr. 1973), no. 48.

[54] See General Instruction of the Roman Missal, nos. 42, 338. *The Roman Ritual* as revised by decree of the Second Vatican Ecumenical Council and published by authority of Pope Paul VI, *Rite of Marriage* (1969; Eng. tr. 1969), nos. 22, 42, 57; *Rite of Funerals* (1969; Eng. tr. 1970), nos. 41, 64.

[55] See General Instruction of the Roman Missal, no. 97.

[56] See ibid., no. 139.

[57] See ibid., no. 23.

[58] See ibid., no. 43.

assembly of the faithful prays in the general intercessions as a rule for the needs of the universal Church and the local community, for the salvation of the world and those oppressed by any burden, and for special categories of people.

The celebrant introduces the prayer; the deacon, another minister, or some of the faithful may propose intentions that are short and phrased with a measure of flexibility. In these petitions "the people, exercising their priestly function, make intercession for all,"[59] with the result that, as the liturgy of the word has its full effects in them, they are better prepared to proceed to the liturgy of the eucharist.

31. For the general intercessions the celebrant presides at the chair and the intentions are announced at the lectern.[60]

The congregation takes part in the general intercessions while standing and by saying or singing a common response after each intention or by silent prayer.[61]

2. AIDS TO THE PROPER CELEBRATION OF THE LITURGY OF THE WORD

a) Place for Proclaiming the Word of God

32. There must be a place in the church that is somewhat elevated, fixed, and of a suitable design and nobility. It should reflect the dignity of God's word and be a clear reminder to the people that in the Mass the table of God's word and of Christ's body is placed before them.[62] The place for the readings must also truly help the people's listening and attention during the liturgy of the word. Great pains must therefore be taken, in keeping with the design of each church, over the harmonious and close relationship of the lectern with the altar.

33. Either permanently or at least on occasions of greater solemnity, the lectern should be decorated simply and in keeping with its design.

Since the lectern is the place from which the ministers proclaim the word of God, it must of its nature be reserved for the readings, the responsorial psalm, and the Easter proclamation (*Exsultet*). The lectern may rightly be used for the homily and the general intercessions, however, because of their close connection with the entire liturgy of the word. It is better for the commentator, cantor,

---

[59] See ibid., no. 45.

[60] See ibid., no. 99.

[61] See ibid., no. 47.

[62] See note 23 of this Introduction.

or director of singing, for example, not to use the lectern.[63]

34. In order that the lectern may properly serve its liturgical purpose, it is to be rather large, since on occasion several ministers must use it at the same time. Provision must also be made for the readers to have enough light to read the text and, as required, to have sound equipment enabling the congregation to hear them without difficulty.

b) *Books for Proclamation of the Word of God*

35. Along with the ministers, the actions, the lectern, and other elements, the books containing the readings of the word of God remind the hearers of the presence of God speaking to his people. Since, in liturgical celebrations the books too serve as signs and symbols of the sacred, care must be taken to ensure that they truly are worthy and beautiful.[64]

36. The proclamation of the gospel always stands as the high point of the liturgy of the word. Thus the liturgical traditions of both the East and the West have consistently continued to preserve some distinction between the books for the readings. The Book of the Gospels was always designed with the utmost care and was more ornate and shown greater respect than any of the other books of readings. In our times also, then, it is very desirable that cathedrals and at least the larger, more populous parishes and the churches with a larger attendance possess a beautifully designed Book of the Gospels, separate from the other book of readings. For good reason it is the Book of the Gospels that is presented to the deacon at his ordination and that is laid upon the head of the bishop-elect and held there at his ordination.[65]

37. Because of the dignity of the word of God, the books of readings used in the celebration are not to be replaced by other pastoral aids, for example, by leaflets printed for the faithful's preparation of the readings or for their personal meditation.

---

[63] See General Instruction of the Roman Missal, no. 272.

[64] See Vatican Council II, Constitution on the Liturgy, no. 122.

[65] See *The Roman Pontifical* revised by decree of the Second Vatican Ecumenical Council and published by authority of Pope Paul VI, *Ordination of Deacons, Priests, and Bishops* (1968; Eng. tr. 1976): *Ordination of Deacons*, no. 24; *Ordination of Deacons and Priests*, no. 21; *Ordination of a Deacon*, no. 24; *Ordination of a Bishop*, no. 25; *Ordination of Bishops*, no. 25.

CHAPTER III

OFFICES AND MINISTRIES IN THE CELEBRATION OF THE LITURGY OF THE WORD WITHIN MASS

1. FUNCTION OF THE ONE PRESIDING AT THE LITURGY OF THE WORD

38. The one presiding at the liturgy of the word brings the spiritual nourishment it contains to those present, especially in the homily. Even if he too is a listener to the word of God proclaimed by others, the duty of proclaiming it has been entrusted above all to him. Personally or through others he sees to it that the word of God is properly proclaimed. He then as a rule reserves to himself the task of composing comments to help the people to listen more attentively and to preach a homily that fosters in them a richer understanding of the word of God.

39. The first requirement for one who is to preside over the celebration is a thorough knowledge of the structure of the Order of Readings so that he will know how to inspire good effects in the hearts of the faithful. Through study and prayer he must also develop a full understanding of the coordination and connection of the various texts in the liturgy of the word, so that the Order of Readings will become the source of a sound understanding of the mystery of Christ and his saving work.

40. The one presiding is to make ready use of the various options provided in the Lectionary regarding readings, responses, responsorial psalms, and gospel acclamations;[66] but he is to do so with

---

[66] See nos. 78–91 of this Introduction.

the agreement[67] of all concerned and after listening to the faithful in regard to what belongs to them.[68]

41. The one presiding exercises his proper office and the ministry of the word of God also as he preaches the homily.[69] In this way he leads his brothers and sisters to an affective knowledge of holy Scripture. He opens their souls to gratitude for the wonderful works of God. He strengthens their faith in the word that in the celebration becomes a sacrament through the Holy Spirit. Finally, he prepares them for a fruitful reception of communion and invites them to embrace the demands of the Christian life.

42. The one presiding is responsible for preparing the faithful for the liturgy of the word on occasion by means of introductions before the readings.[70] These comments can help the gathered assembly toward a better hearing of the word of God, because they enliven the people's faith and their desire for good. He may also carry out this responsibility through other persons, the deacon, for example, or a commentator.[71]

43. As he directs the general intercessions and through their introduction and conclusion connects them, if possible, with the day's readings and the homily, the one presiding leads the faithful toward the liturgy of the eucharist.[72]

2. ROLE OF THE FAITHFUL IN THE LITURGY OF THE WORD

44. Christ's word gathers the people of God as one and increases and sustains them. "This applies above all to the liturgy of the word in the celebration of Mass: there is an inseparable union between the proclamation of the death of the Lord, the response of the people listening, and the offering through which Christ has confirmed the New Covenant in his blood. The people share in this offering by their inner intentions and the reception of the sacrament."[73] For "not only when things are read 'that were written for our instruction' (Romans 15:4), but also when the Church prays or sings or acts, the faith of those taking part is nourished and their minds are raised to God, so that they may offer him their worship

---

[67] See General Instruction of the Roman Missal, nos. 318–320; 324–325.

[68] See ibid., no. 313.

[69] See ibid., no. 42. Congregation for the Sacraments and Divine Worship, instruction *Inaestimabile Donum*, 3 April 1980, no. 3: AAS 72 (1980) 334.

[70] See General Instruction of the Roman Missal, no. 11.

[71] See ibid., no. 68.

[72] See ibid., nos. 33, 47.

[73] Vatican Council II, Decree on the Ministry and Life of Priests, no. 4.

as intelligent beings and receive his grace more abundantly."[74]

45. In the liturgy of the word, the congregation of the faithful still today receives from God the word of his covenant through the faith that comes by hearing. The faithful must respond to that word in the same faith so that more and more they may become the people of the New Covenant.

The people of God have a spiritual right to receive abundantly from the treasury of God's word. Its riches are presented to them through use of the Order of Readings, the homily, and pastoral efforts.

For their part, the faithful at the celebration of Mass are to listen to the word of God with an inward and outward reverence that will bring them continuous growth in the spiritual life and draw them more deeply into the mystery they celebrate.[75]

46. As a help toward celebrating the memorial of the Lord with devotion, the faithful should be keenly aware of the one presence of Christ in both the word of God—"it is he who speaks when the holy Scriptures are read in the Church"—and "especially under the eucharistic elements."[76]

47. To be received and integrated into the life of Christ's faithful, the word of God demands a living faith.[77] Hearing the word of God unceasingly proclaimed arouses that faith.

The Scriptures, and above all in their liturgical proclamation, are the source of life and power. As Paul attests, the Gospel is the saving power of God for everyone who believes.[78] Love of the Scriptures is therefore the force that renews the entire people of God.[79] All the faithful without exception must therefore always be ready to listen gladly to God's word.[80] When this word is proclaimed in the Church and put into living practice, it enlightens the faithful through the working of the Holy Spirit and draws them into the entire mystery of the Lord as a reality to be lived.[81] The word of God reverently received moves the heart and its desires toward conversion and toward a life filled with both individual and com-

---

[74] Vatican Council II, Constitution on the Liturgy, no. 33.

[75] See General Instruction of the Roman Missal, no. 9.

[76] Vatican Council II, Constitution on the Liturgy, no. 7.

[77] See ibid., no. 9.

[78] See Romans 1:16.

[79] See Vatican Council II, Dogmatic Constitution on Divine Revelation, no. 21.

[80] See ibid.

[81] See John 14:15–26; 15:26–16:4, 5–15.

munity faith,[82] since God's word is the sustenance of the Christian life and the source of the prayer of the entire Church.[83]

48. The close connection between the liturgy of the word and the liturgy of the eucharist in the Mass should prompt the faithful to be present right from the beginning of the celebration,[84] to take part attentively, and to dispose themselves to hear the word, especially by learning beforehand more about Scripture. That same connection should also awaken in them a desire for a liturgical understanding of the texts read and for the willingness to respond through singing.[85]

When they hear the word of God and reflect deeply on it, the faithful receive the power to respond to it actively with full faith, hope, and charity through prayer and self-giving, and not only during Mass but in their entire Christian life.

3. MINISTRIES IN THE LITURGY OF THE WORD

49. Liturgical tradition assigns responsibility for the biblical readings in the celebration of Mass to ministers: to readers and the deacon. But when there is no deacon or another priest present, the priest celebrant is to read the gospel[86] and when there is no reader present, all the readings.[87]

50. The deacon's part in the liturgy of the word at Mass is to proclaim the gospel, sometimes to give the homily, as occasion suggests, and to propose the intentions of the general intercessions to the people.[88]

51. "The reader has his own proper function in the eucharistic celebration and should exercise this even though ministers of a higher rank may be present."[89] The reader's ministry, which is

---

[82] See Vatican Council II, Decree on the Missionary Activity of the Church, nos. 6 and 15; also Dogmatic Constitution on Divine Revelation, no. 26.

[83] See Vatican Council II, Constitution on the Liturgy, no. 24. See also Congregation for the Clergy, *Directorium catechisticum generale,* 11 April 1971, no. 25: AAS 64 (1972) 114.

[84] See Vatican Council II, Constitution on the Liturgy, no. 56. See also Congregation for the Sacraments and Divine Worship, instruction *Inaestimabile Donum,* 3 April 1980, no. 1: AAS 72 (1980) 333–334.

[86] See Vatican Council II, Constitution on the Liturgy, nos. 24 and 35.

[86] See General Instruction of the Roman Missal, no. 34.

[87] See ibid., no. 96.

[88] See ibid., nos. 47, 61, 132; Congregation for the Sacraments and Divine Worship, instruction *Inaestimabile Donum,* 3 April 1980, no. 3: AAS 72 (1980) 334.

[89] General Instruction of the Roman Missal, no. 66.

conferred through a liturgical rite, must be held in respect. When there are instituted readers available, they are to carry out their office at least on Sundays and major feasts, especially at the principal Mass of the day. These readers may also be given responsibility for assisting in the planning of the liturgy of the word, and, to the extent necessary, of seeing to the preparation of others of the faithful who may be appointed on a given occasion to serve as readers at Mass.[90]

52. The liturgical assembly truly requires readers, even those not instituted. Proper measures must therefore be taken to ensure that there are qualified laypersons who have been trained to carry out this ministry.[91] Whenever there is more than one reading, it is better to assign the readings to different readers, if available.

53. In Masses without a deacon, the function of announcing the intentions for the general intercessions is to be assigned to the cantor, particularly when they are to be sung, to a reader, or to another person.[92]

54. During the celebration of Mass with a congregation a second priest, a deacon, and an instituted reader must wear the distinctive vestment of their office when they go to the lectern to read the word of God. Those who carry out the ministry of reader just for the occasion or even regularly but without institution may go to the lectern in ordinary attire that is in keeping with local custom.

55. "It is necessary that those who exercise the ministry of reader, even if they have not received institution, be truly qualified and carefully prepared so that the faithful may develop a warm and living love for Scripture from listening to the sacred texts read."[93]

Their preparation must above all be spiritual, but what may be called a technical preparation is also needed. The spiritual preparation presupposes at least a biblical and liturgical formation. The purpose of their biblical formation is to give readers the ability to understand the readings in context and to perceive by the light of faith the central point of the revealed message. The

---

[90] See Paul VI, motu proprio *Ministeria quaedam*, 15 Aug. 1972, no. V: AAS 64 (1972) 532.

[91] See Congregation for the Sacraments and Divine Worship, instruction *Inaestimabile Donum*, 3 April 1980, nos. 2 and 18: AAS 72 (1980) 334 and 338. See also Congregation for Divine Worship, *Directory for Masses with Children* (1973; Eng. tr. 1973), nos. 22, 24, 27.

[92] See General Instruction of the Roman Missal, nos. 47, 66, 151. See also Consilium, *De oratione communi seu fidelium* (Vatican City, 1966), no. 8.

[93] General Instruction of the Roman Missal, no. 66.

liturgical formation ought to equip the readers to have some grasp of the meaning and structure of the liturgy of the word and of the significance of its connection with the liturgy of the eucharist. The technical preparation should make the readers more skilled in the art of reading publicly, either with the power of their own voice or with the help of sound equipment.

56. The psalmist, that is the cantor of the psalm, is responsible for singing, responsorially or directly, the chants between the readings—the psalm or other biblical canticle, the gradual and *Alleluia*, or other chant. The psalmist may, as occasion requires, intone the *Alleluia* and verse.[94]

For carrying out the function of psalmist it is advantageous to have in each ecclesial community laypersons with a talent for singing and correct diction. The points made about the formation of readers apply to cantor as well.

57. The commentator also fulfills a genuine liturgical ministry, which consists in presenting to the assembly of the faithful, from a suitable place, relevant explanations and comments that are clear, of marked simplicity, meticulously prepared, as a rule written out, and approved beforehand by the celebrant.[95]

---

[94] See General Instruction of the Roman Missal, nos. 37a and 67.

[95] See ibid., no. 68.

PART TWO

STRUCTURE OF THE ORDER OF READINGS FOR MASS

CHAPTER IV

GENERAL PLAN OF THE READINGS FOR MASS

1. PASTORAL AIM OF THE ORDER OF READINGS FOR MASS

58. On the basis of the intention of Vatican Council II, the Order of Readings provided by the Lectionary of the Roman Missal has been composed above all for a pastoral purpose. To achieve this aim, not only the principles underlying this new Order of Readings but also the lists of texts that it provides have been discussed and revised over and over again, with the cooperation of a great many experts in exegesis, pastoral studies, catechetics, and liturgy from all parts of the world. The Order of Readings is the fruit of this combined effort.

The prolonged use of this Order of Readings to proclaim and explain sacred Scripture in the eucharistic celebration will, it is hoped, prove to be an effective step toward achieving the objective stated repeatedly by Vatican Council II.[96]

---

[96] See for example Paul VI, apostolic constitution *Missale Romanum:* "All this has been planned to develop among the faithful a greater hunger for the word of

59. The decision on revising the Lectionary for Mass was to draw up and edit a single, rich, and full Order of Readings that would be in complete accord with the intent and prescriptions of the Council.[97] At the same time, however, the Order was meant to be of a kind that would meet the requirements and usages of particular Churches and liturgical assemblies. For this reason, those responsible for the revision took pains to safeguard the liturgical tradition of the Roman Rite, but valued highly the merits of all the systems of selecting, arranging, and using the biblical readings in other liturgical families and in certain particular Churches. The revisers made use of those elements that experience has confirmed, but with an effort to avoid certain shortcomings found in the preceding form of the tradition.

60. The present Order of Readings for Mass, then, is an arrangement of biblical readings that provides the faithful with a knowledge of the whole of God's word, in a pattern suited to the purpose. Throughout the liturgical year, but above all during the seasons of Easter, Lent, and Advent, the choice and sequence of readings are aimed at giving the faithful an ever-deepening perception of the faith they profess and of the history of salvation.[98] Accordingly, the Order of Readings corresponds to the requirements and interests of the Christian people.

61. The celebration of the liturgy is not in itself simply a form of catechesis, but it does contain an element of teaching. The Lectionary of the Roman Missal brings this out[99] and therefore deserves to be regarded as a pedagogical resource aiding catechesis.

God. Under the guidance of the Holy Spirit, this hunger will seem, so to speak, to impel the people of the New Covenant toward the perfect unity of the Church. We are fully confident on this account that both priests and faithful will prepare their minds and hearts more devoutly for the Lord's Supper and that, meditating on the Scriptures, they will be nourished more each day by the words of the Lord. In accord with the hopes of Vatican Council II, all will thus regard sacred Scripture as the abiding source of spiritual life, the foundation for Christian instruction, and the core of all theological study" (in *The Roman Missal*).

[97] See Vatican Council II, Constitution on the Liturgy, nos. 35 and 51.

[98] See Paul VI, apostolic constitution *Missale Romanum*: "This is meant to provide a fuller exposition of the continuing process of the mystery of salvation as shown in the words of divine revelation" (in *The Roman Missal*).

[99] See Vatican Council II, Constitution on the Liturgy, nos. 9, 33. Congregation of Rites, instruction *Inter Oecumenici*, 26 Sept. 1964, no. 7: AAS 56 (1964) 878. John Paul II, apostolic exhortation *Catechesi tradendae*, 16 Oct. 1979, no. 23: AAS 71 (1979) 1296–1297.

This is so because the Order of Readings for Mass aptly presents from Scripture the principal deeds and words belonging to the history of salvation. As its many phases and events are recalled in the liturgy of the word, the faithful will come to see that the history of salvation is contained here and now in the representation of Christ's paschal mystery celebrated through the eucharist.

62. The pastoral advantage of having in the Roman Rite a single Order of Readings for the Lectionary is obvious on other grounds. All the faithful, particularly those who for various reasons do not always take part in Mass with the same assembly, will everywhere be able to hear the same readings on any given day or in any liturgical season and to reflect on the application of these readings to their own circumstances. This is the case even in places that have no priest and where a deacon or someone else deputed by the bishop conducts a celebration of the word of God.[100]

63. Pastors may wish to respond specifically from the word of God to the concerns of their own congregations. Although they must be mindful that they are above all to be the heralds of the entire mystery of Christ and the Gospel, they may rightfully use the options provided in the Order of Readings for Mass. This applies particularly to the celebration of a ritual or votive Mass, a Mass in honor of the saints, or one of the Masses for various needs and occasions. In the light of the general norms, special faculties are granted for the readings in Masses with particular groups.[101]

2. PRINCIPLES USED IN DRAWING UP THE ORDER OF READINGS FOR MASS

64. To achieve the purpose of the Order of Readings for Mass, the parts have been selected and arranged in such a way as to take into account the sequence of the liturgical seasons and the hermeneutical principles discovered and formulated through contemporary biblical research.

It was judged helpful to state here the principles guiding the composition of the Order of Readings for Mass.

a) Selection of Texts

65. The course of readings in the Proper of Seasons is arranged as follows. Sundays and the solemnities of the Lord present the more

---

[100] See Vatican Council II, Constitution on the Liturgy, no. 35, 4. Congregation of Rites, instruction *Inter Oecumenici*, 26 Sept. 1964, nos. 37–38: AAS 56 (1964) 884.

[101] See Congregation for Divine Worship, instruction *Actio pastoralis*, 15 May 1969, no. 6: AAS 61 (1969) 809; *Directory for Masses with Children* (1973; Eng. tr. 1973), nos. 41–47. Paul VI, apostolic exhortation *Marialis cultus*, 2 Feb. 1974, no. 12: AAS 66 (1974) 125–126.

important biblical passages. In this way the more significant parts
of God's revealed word can be read to the assembly of the faithful
within a reasonable period of time. Weekdays present a second
series of texts from Scripture and in a sense these complement the
message of salvation explained on Sundays and the solemnities of
the Lord. But neither series in these main parts of the Order of
Readings—the series for Sundays and the solemnities of the Lord
and for weekdays—depends on the other. The Order of Readings
for Sundays and the solemnities of the Lord extends over three
years; for weekdays, over two. Thus each runs its course in-
dependently of the other.

The course of readings in other parts of the Order of Readings is
governed by its own rules. This applies to the series of readings for
celebrations of the saints, ritual Masses, Masses for various needs
and occasions, votive Masses, or Masses for the dead.

*b) Arrangement of the Readings for Sundays and Solemnities
of the Lord*

66. The following are features proper to the readings for Sundays
and the solemnities of the Lord:

1. Each Mass has three readings: the first from the Old Testament, the second from an apostle (that is, either from a letter or from Revelation, depending on the season), and the
third from the gospels. This arrangement brings out the
unity of the Old and New Testaments and of the history of
salvation, in which Christ is the central figure, com-
memorated in his paschal mystery.
2. A more varied and richer reading of Scripture on Sundays
and the solemnities of the Lord results from the three-year
cycle provided for these days, in that the same texts are
read only every fourth year.[102]

---

[102] Each of the years is designated by a letter, A, B, or C. The following is the procedure to determine which year is A, B, or C. The letter C designates a year whose
number is divisible into three equal parts, as though the cycle had taken its beginning from the first year of the Christian era. Thus the year 1 would have been Year
A; year 2, Year B; year 3, Year C, (as would years 6, 9, and 12). Thus, for example,
year 1980 is Year C; 1981, Year A; 1982, Year B; and 1983, Year C again. And so
forth. Obviously each cycle runs in accord with the plan of the liturgical year, that
is, it begins with the First Week of Advent, which falls in the preceding year of the
civil calendar.

The distinguishing characteristics for the years in each cycle is based in a sense
on the principal note of the Synoptic Gospel used for the semicontinuous reading
of Ordinary Time. Thus the first Year of the cycle is the Year for the reading of the
Gospel of Matthew and is so named; the second and third Years are the Year of
Mark and the Year of Luke.

3. The principles governing the Order of Readings for Sundays and the solemnities of the Lord are called the principles of "harmony" and of "semicontinuous reading." One or the other applies according to the different seasons of the year and the distinctive character of the particular liturgical season.

67. The best instance of harmony between the Old and New Testament readings occurs when it is one that Scripture itself suggests. This is the case when the teaching and events recounted in texts of the New Testament bear a more or less explicit relationship to the teaching and events of the Old Testament. The present Order of Readings selects Old Testament texts mainly because of their correlation with New Testament texts read in the same Mass, and particularly with the gospel text.

Harmony of another kind exists between texts of the readings for each Mass during Advent, Lent, and Easter, the seasons that have a distinctive importance or character.

In contrast, the Sundays in Ordinary Time do not have a distinctive character. Thus the texts of both the apostolic and gospel readings are arranged in an order of semicontinuous reading, whereas the Old Testament reading is harmonized with the gospel.

68. The decision was made not to extend to Sundays the arrangement suited to the liturgical seasons mentioned, that is, not to have an organic harmony of themes designed to aid homiletic instruction. Such an arrangement would be in conflict with the genuine conception of liturgical celebration. The liturgy is always the celebration of the mystery of Christ and makes use of the word of God on the basis of its own tradition, guided not by merely logical or extrinsic concerns but by the desire to proclaim the Gospel and to lead those who believe to the fullness of truth.

c) Arrangement of the Readings for Weekdays

69. The weekday readings have been arranged in the following way:

1. Each Mass has two readings: the first is from the Old Testament or from an apostle (from a letter or Revelation), and during the Easter season from Acts; the second, from the gospels.

2. The yearly cycle for Lent has its proper principles of arrangement, which take into account the baptismal and penitential themes of this season.

3. The cycle for the weekdays of Advent, the Christmas season, and the Easter season is also yearly and the readings thus remain the same each year.

4. For the thirty-four weeks of Ordinary Time, the gospel readings are arranged in a single cycle, repeated each year. But the first reading is arranged in a two-year cycle and is thus read every other year. Year I is used during odd-numbered years; Year II, during even-numbered years.

Like the Order for Sundays and the solemnities of the Lord, then, the weekday Order of Readings is governed by similar application of the principles of harmony and of semicontinuous reading, especially in the case of seasons with their own distinctive character.

d) Readings for Celebrations of the Saints

70. Two groups of readings are provided for celebrations of the saints:

1. The proper of Saints provides the first group, for solemnities, feasts, or memorials and particularly when there are proper texts for such celebrations. Sometimes in the Proper, however, there is a reference to the most appropriate among the texts in the Commons as the one to be given preference.
2. The Commons of Saints provide the second, more extensive group of readings. There are, first, appropriate texts for the different classes of saints (martyrs, pastors, virgins, etc.), then a great many texts that deal with holiness in general. These are for alternative use whenever the Commons are indicated as the source for the choice of readings.

71. As to their sequence, all the texts in this part of the Order of Readings appear in the order in which they are to be read at Mass. Thus the Old Testament texts are first, then the texts of an apostle, followed by the psalms and verses between the readings, and finally the texts from the gospels. The rationale of this arrangement is that, unless otherwise noted, the celebrant may choose at will from such texts, in view of the pastoral needs of the assembly taking part in the celebration.

e) Readings for Ritual Masses, Masses for Various Needs and Occasions, Votive Masses, and Masses for the Dead

72. For ritual Masses, Masses for various needs and occassions, votive Masses, and Masses for the dead, the texts for the readings are arranged as just described, that is, many texts are grouped together in the order of their use, as in the Commons of Saints.

f) Main Criteria Applied in Choosing and Arranging the Readings

73. In addition to the guiding principles already given for the arrangement of readings in the individual parts of the Order of Readings, others of a more general nature are:

1) Reservation of some books on the basis of the liturgical seasons

74. In this Order of Readings, some biblical books are set aside for particular liturgical seasons on the basis of both the intrinsic importance of subject matter and liturgical tradition. For example, the Western (Ambrosian and Hispanic) and Eastern tradition of reading Acts during Easter season is respected. This usage results in a clear presentation of how the Church derives the beginning of its entire life from the paschal mystery. Another tradition of both West and East that is retained is the reading of the Gospel of John in the latter weeks of Lent and in the Easter season.

Tradition assigns the reading of Isaiah, especially the first part, to Advent. Some texts of this book, however, are read during the Christmas season, to which 1 John is also assigned.

2) Length of texts

75. A *via media* is followed in regard to the length of texts. A distinction has been made between narratives, which require reading a fairly long passage but which usually hold the people's attention, and texts that should not be lengthy because of the profundity of their teaching.

In the case of certain rather long texts, longer and shorter versions are provided to suit different situations. The editing of the shorter version has been carried out with great caution.

3) Difficult texts

76. In readings for Sundays and solemnities, texts that present real difficulties are avoided for pastoral reasons. The difficulties may be objective, in that the texts themselves raise complex literary, critical, or exegetical problems; or, at least to a certain extent, the difficulties may lie in the faithful's ability to understand the texts. But there could be no justification for depriving the faithful of the spiritual riches of certain texts on the grounds of difficulty if its source is the inadequacy either of the religious education that every Christian should have or of the biblical formation that every pastor should have. Often a difficult reading is clarified by its correlation with another in the same Mass.

4) Omission of texts

77. The omission of verses in reading from Scripture has at times been the practice in many liturgical traditions, including the

Roman. Admittedly such omissions may not be made lightly, for fear of distorting the meaning of the text or the intent and style of Scripture. Yet on pastoral grounds it was decided to continue the tradition in the present Order of Readings, but at the same time to ensure that the essential meaning of the text remained intact. One reason for the decision is that otherwise some texts would have been unduly long. It would also have been necessary to omit completely certain readings of high spiritual value for the faithful because those readings include some verse that is unsuitable pastorally or that involves truely difficult problems.

3. PRINCIPLES TO BE FOLLOWED IN THE USE
OF THE ORDER OF READINGS

a) Options in the Choice of Some Texts

78. The Order of Readings sometimes leaves it to the celebrant to choose between alternative texts or to choose one from the several listed together for the same reading. The option seldom exists on Sundays, solemnities, or the greater feasts in order not to obscure the proper character of the particular liturgical season or needlessly interrupt the semicontinuous reading of some biblical book. On the other hand, the option is given readily in celebrations of the saints, in ritual Masses, Masses for various needs and occasions, votive Masses, and Masses for the dead.

These options, together with those indicated in the General Instruction of the Roman Missal and the *Ordo cantus Missae*,[103] have a pastoral aim. In planning the liturgy of the word, then, the priest should consider "the general spiritual good of the assembly rather than his personal outlook. He should be mindful that the choice of texts is to be made in consultation with the ministers and others who have a function in the celebration and should listen to the faithful in regard to the parts that more directly belong to them."[104]

1) The two readings before the gospel

79. In Masses assigned three readings, the three are to be used. If, however, for pastoral reasons the conference of bishops has permitted use of only two readings,[105] the choice between the two first

---

[103]See General Instruction of the Roman Missal, nos. 36-40. *Missale Romanum ex Decreto Sacrosancti Oecumenici Concilii Vaticani II instauratum, auctoritate Pauli Pp. VI promulgatum, Ordo cantus Missae*, (Vatican Polyglot Press, 1972) *Praenotanda*, nos. 5-9.

[104]General Instruction of the Roman Missal, no. 313.

[105]See ibid., no. 318; Congregation for the Sacraments and Divine Worship, instruction *Inaestimabile Donum*, 3 April 1980, no. 1: AAS 72 (1980) 333-334.

readings is to be made in such a way as to safeguard the Church's intent to instruct the faithful more completely in the mystery of salvation. Thus, unless the contrary is indicated in the text of the Lectionary, the reading to be chosen as the first reading is the one that is closer to the theme of the gospel, or, in accord with the intent just mentioned, that is more helpful toward a coherent catechesis over an extended period, or that preserves the semicontinuous reading of some biblical book.[106]

2) Long and short forms of texts

80. A pastoral criterion must also guide the choice between the longer and shorter forms of a text. The main consideration must be the capacity of the hearers to listen profitably either to the longer or to the shorter reading; or to listen to a more complete text that will be explained through the homily.

3) When two texts are provided

81. When a choice is allowed between alternative texts, whether they are fixed or optional, the first consideration must be the best interests of those taking part. It may be a matter of using the easier text or the one more relevant to the gathered assembly or, as pastoral advantage may suggest, of repeating or replacing a text that is assigned as proper to one celebration and optional to another.

The issue may arise when it is feared that some text will create difficulties for a particular congregation or when the same text would have to be repeated within a few days, as on a Sunday and on a following weekday.

4) Weekday readings

82. The arrangement of weekday readings provides texts for every day of the week throughout the year. In most cases, therefore, these readings are to be used on their assigned days, unless a solemnity, feast, or memorial with proper readings occurs.[107]

The one using the Order of Readings for weekdays must check

---

[106]For example: in Lent the continuity of the Old Testament readings corresponds to the unfolding of the history of salvation; the Sundays in Ordinary Time provide the semicontinuous reading of one of the letters of the apostles. In these cases it is right that the priest choose one or other of the readings in a systematic way over a series of Sundays so that he may set up a coherent plan for catechesis. It is not right to read indiscriminately on one day from the Old Testament, or another from the letter of an apostle, without any orderly plan for subsequent texts.

[107]See General Instruction of the Roman Missal, no. 319.

to see whether one reading or another from the same biblical book will have to be omitted because of some celebration occurring during the week. With the plan of readings for the entire week in mind, the priest in that case arranges to omit the less significant selections or suitably combines them with other readings, if they contribute to an integral view of a particular theme.

5) Celebrations of the saints

83. When they exist, proper readings are given for celebrations of the saints, that is, biblical passages about the saint or the event in the saint's life that the Mass is celebrating. Even in the case of a memorial these readings must take the place of the weekday readings for the same day. This Order of Readings makes explicit note of every case of proper readings on a memorial.

In some cases there are accommodated readings, those, namely, that bring out some particular aspect of a saint's spiritual life or apostolate. Use of such readings does not seem binding, except for compelling pastoral reasons. For the most part references are given to readings in the Commons in order to facilitate choice. But these are merely suggestions: in place of an accommodated reading or the particular reading proposed from a Common, any other reading from the Commons referred to may be selected.

The first concern of a priest celebrating with a congregation is the spiritual benefit of the faithful and he will be careful not to impose his personal preference on them. Above all he will make sure not to omit too often or needlessly the readings assigned for each day in the weekday Lectionary: the Church's desire is to provide the faithful with a richer share at the table of God's word.[108]

There are also general readings, that is, those placed in the Commons either for some determined class of saints (martyrs, virgins, pastors, etc.) or for the saints in general. Because in these cases several texts are listed for the same reading, it will be up to the priest to choose the one best suited to the congregation.

In all celebrations of saints the readings may be taken not only from the Common to which references are given in each case, but also from the Common of Holy Men and Women, whenever there is special reason for doing so.

84. For celebrations of the saints:

> a. On solemnities and feasts the readings must be those that are given in the Proper or the Commons. For solemnities and feasts of the General Roman Calendar proper readings are always assigned.

---

[108]See ibid., no. 316c. Vatican Council II, Constitution on the Liturgy, no. 51.

b. On solemnities belonging to particular calendars, three readings are to be assigned, unless the conference of bishops has decreed that there are to be only two readings.[109] The first reading is from the Old Testament (but during the Easter season, from Acts or Revelation); the second, from an apostle; the third, from the gospels.

c. On feasts and memorials, which have only two readings, the first can be chosen from either the Old Testament or from an apostle; the second is from the gospels. Following the Church's traditional practice, however, the first reading during the Easter season is to be taken from an apostle, the second, as far as possible, from the Gospel of John.

6) Other Parts of the Order of Readings

85. In the Order of Readings for ritual Masses the references given are to the texts already published for the individual rites. This obviously does not include the texts belonging to celebrations that must not be integrated with Mass.[110]

86. The Order of Readings for Masses for various needs and occasions, votive Masses, and Masses for the dead provides many texts that can be of assistance in adapting such celebrations to the situation, circumstances, and concerns of the particular groups taking part.[111]

87. In ritual Masses, Masses for various needs and occasions, votive Masses, and Masses for the dead, since many texts are given for the same reading, the choice of readings follows the criteria already indicated for the choice of readings from the Common of Saints.

88. On a day when some ritual Mass is not permitted and the norms in the individual rite allow the choice of one reading from those provided for ritual Masses, the general spiritual welfare of the participants must be the primary consideration.[112]

b) *Responsorial Psalm and Acclamation Before the Gospel*

89. Among the chants between the readings, the psalm after the first reading is very important. As a rule the psalm to be used is the one assigned to the reading. But in the case of readings for the

---

[109]See General Instruction of the Roman Missal, no. 318.

[110]See *The Roman Ritual* as revised by decree of the Second Vatican Ecumenical Council and published by authority of Pope Paul VI, *Rite of Penance* (1974 Eng. tr. 1974), Introduction, no. 13.

[111]See General Instruction of the Roman Missal, no. 320.

[112]See ibid., no. 313.

Common of Saints, ritual Masses, Masses for various needs and occasions, votive Masses, and masses for the dead the choice is left
up to the priest celebrating. He will base his choice on the principle of the pastoral benefit of those participating.

But to make it easier for the people to join in the response to the
psalm, the Order of Readings lists certain other texts of psalms
and responses that have been chosen according to the various
seasons or classes of saints. Whenever the psalm is sung, these
texts may replace the text corresponding to the reading.[113]

90. The chant between the second reading and the gospel is either
specified in each Mass and correlated with the gospel or else it is
left as a choice to be made from those in the series belonging to a
liturgical season or to one of the Commons.

91. During Lent one of the acclamations from those given in the
text of the Order of Readings[114] may be used, depending on the occasion. This acclamation is made before and after the verse before
the gospel.

> [The forms customary for this acclamation are:
> Praise to you, Lord Jesus Christ, king of endless glory!
> Praise and honor to you, Lord Jesus Christ!
> Glory and praise to you, Lord Jesus Christ!
> Glory to you, Word of God, Lord Jesus Christ!]

---

[113]See nos. 173-174 of this Order of Readings.

[114]See no. 223 of this Order of Readings.

CHAPTER V

DESCRIPTION OF THE ORDER OF READINGS

92. It seems useful to provide here a brief description of the Order of Readings, at least for the principal celebrations and the different seasons of the liturgical year. With these in mind, readings were selected on the basis of the rules already stated. This description is meant to assist priests to understand the structure of the Order of Readings so that their use of it will become more perceptive and the Order of Readings a source of good for Christ's faithful.

1. ADVENT

a) Sundays

93. Each gospel reading has a distinctive theme: the Lord's coming at the end of time (First Sunday of Advent), John the Baptist (Second and Third Sunday), and the events that prepared immediately for the Lord's birth (Fourth Sunday).

The Old Testament readings are prophecies about the Messiah and the Messianic age, especially from Isaiah.

The readings from an apostle serve as exhortations and as proclamations, in keeping with the different themes of Advent.

b) Weekdays

94. There are two series of readings: one to be used from the beginning of Advent until 16 December; the other from 17 to 24 December.

In the first part of Advent there are readings from Isaiah, distributed in accord with the sequence of the book itself and including salient texts that are also read on the Sundays. For the choice of the weekday gospel the first reading has been taken into consideration.

On Thursday of the second week the readings of the gospel about John the Baptist begin. The first reading is either a continuation of Isaiah or a text chosen in view of the gospel.

In the last week before Christmas the events that immediately prepared for the Lord's birth are presented from Matthew (Chapter 1) and Luke (Chapter 1). The texts in the first reading, chosen in view of the gospel reading, are from different Old Testament books and include important Messianic prophecies.

2) CHRISTMAS SEASON

a) Solemnities, Feasts, and Sundays

95. For the vigil and the three Masses of Christmas both the prophetic readings and the others have been chosen from the Roman tradition.

The gospel on the Sunday within the octave of Christmas, feast of the Holy Family, is about Jesus' childhood and the other readings are about the virtues of family life.

On the octave of Christmas, solemnity of Mary, Mother of God, the readings are about the Virgin Mother of God and the giving of the holy Name of Jesus.

On the second Sunday after Christmas, the readings are about the mystery of the incarnation.

On Epiphany, the Old Testament reading and the gospel continue the Roman tradition; the text for the reading from the apostolic letters is about the calling of all people to salvation.

On the feast of the Baptism of the Lord, the texts chosen are about this mystery.

b) Weekdays

96. From 29 December on, there is a continuous reading of the whole of 1 John, which actually begins earlier, on 27 December, feast of St. John the Evangelist, and on 28 December, feast of the Holy Innocents. The gospels relate manifestations of the Lord: events of Jesus' childhood from Luke (29-30 December); passages from John 1 (31 December-5 January); other manifestations from the four gospels (7-18 January).

3. LENT

a) Sundays

97. The gospel readings are arranged as follows:
The first and second Sundays retain the accounts of the Lord's

temptations and transfiguration, with readings, however, from all three Synoptics.

On the next three Sundays, the gospels about the Samaritan woman, the man born blind, and the raising of Lazarus have been restored in Year A. Because these gospels are of major importance in regard to Christian initiation, they may also be read in Year B and Year C, especially in places where there are catechumens.

Other texts, however, are provided for Year B and Year C: for Year B, a text from John about Christ's coming glorification through his cross and resurrection and for Year C, a text from Luke about conversion.

On Passion Sunday (Palm Sunday) the texts for the procession are selections from the Synoptic Gospels concerning the Lord's triumphal entrance into Jerusalem. For the Mass the reading is the account of the Lord's passion.

The Old Testament readings are about the history of salvation, which is one of the themes proper to the catechesis of Lent. The series of texts for each Year presents the main elements of salvation history from its beginning until the promise of the New Covenant.

The readings from the letters of the apostles have been selected to fit the gospel and the Old Testament readings and, to the extent possible, to provide a connection between them.

b) Weekdays

98. The readings from the gospels and the Old Testament were selected because they are related to each other. They treat various themes of the Lenten catechesis that are suited to the spiritual significance of this season. Beginning with Monday of the fourth week of Lent, there is a semicontinuous reading of the Gospel of John, made up of texts that correspond more closely to the themes proper to Lent.

Because the readings about the Samaritan women, the man born blind, and the raising of Lazarus are now assigned to Sundays, but only for Year A (in Year B and Year C they are optional), provision has been made for their use on weekdays. Thus at the beginning of the Third, Fourth, and Fifth Weeks of Lent optional Masses with these texts for the gospel have been inserted and may be used in place of the readings of the day on any weekday of the respective week.

In the first half of Holy Week the readings are about the mystery of Christ's passion. For the chrism Mass the readings bring out both Christ's messianic mission and its continuation in the Church by means of the sacraments.

4. THE EASTER TRIDUUM AND THE EASTER SEASON

a) The Easter Triduum

99. On Holy Thursday at the evening Mass the remembrance of the supper preceding Christ's departure casts its own special light because of the Lord's example in washing the feet of his disciples and Paul's account of the institution of the Christian Passover in the eucharist.

On Good Friday the liturgical service has as its center John's narrative of the passion of him who was portrayed in Isaiah as the Servant of Yahweh and who became the one High Priest by offering himself to the Father.

On the holy night of the Easter Vigil there are seven Old Testament readings, recalling the wonderful works of God in the history of salvation. There are two New Testament readings, the announcement of the resurrection according to one of the Synoptic Gospels and a reading from St. Paul on Christian baptism as the sacrament of Christ's resurrection.

The gospel reading for the Mass on Easter day is from John on the finding of the empty tomb. There is also, however, the option to use the gospel texts from the Easter Vigil or, when there is an evening Mass on Easter Sunday, to use the account in Luke of the Lord's appearance to the disciples on the road to Emmaus. The first reading is from Acts, which throughout the Easter season replaces the Old Testament reading. The reading from St. Paul concerns the living out of the paschal mystery in the Church.

b) Sundays

100. The gospel readings for the first three Sundays recount the appearances of the risen Christ. The readings about the Good Shepherd are assigned to the Fourth Sunday. On the Fifth, Sixth, and Seventh Sundays, there are excerpts from the Lord's discourse and prayer at the last supper.

The first reading is from Acts, in a three-year cycle of parallel and progressive selections: material is presented on the life of the primitive Church, its witness, and its growth.

For the reading from the apostles, 1 Peter is in Year A, 1 John in Year B, Revelation in Year C. These are the texts that seem to fit in especially well with the spirit of joyous faith and sure hope proper to this season.

c) Weekdays

101. As on the Sundays, the first reading is a semicontinuous reading from Acts. The gospel readings during the Easter octave are accounts of the Lord's appearances. After that there is a

semicontinuous reading of the Gospel of John, but with texts that have a paschal character in order to complete the reading from John during Lent. This paschal reading is made up in large part of the Lord's discourse and prayer at the last supper.

d) Solemnities of the Ascension and Pentecost

102. For the first reading the solemnity of the Ascension retains the account of the Ascension according to Acts. This text is complemented by the second reading from the apostolic reflections on Christ in exaltation at the right hand of the Father. For the gospel reading, each of the three Years has its own text in accord with the differences in the Synoptic Gospels.

In the evening Mass celebrated on the vigil of Pentecost four Old Testament texts are provided; any one of them may be used, in order to bring out the many aspects of Pentecost. The reading from the apostles shows the actual working of the Holy Spirit in the Church. The gospel reading recalls the promise of the Spirit made by Christ before his own glorification.

For the Mass on Pentecost itself, in accord with received usage, the account in Acts of the great occurrence on Pentecost is taken as the first reading. The texts from Paul bring out the effect of the action of the Holy Spirit in the life of the Church. The gospel reading is a remembrance of Jesus bestowing his Spirit on the disciples on Easter evening; other optional texts describe the action of the Spirit on the disciples and on the Church.

5. ORDINARY TIME

a) Arrangement and Choice of Texts

103. Ordinary Time begins on the Monday after the Sunday following 6 January; it lasts until the Tuesday before Lent inclusive. It begins again on the Monday after Pentecost Sunday and finishes before evening prayer I of the first Sunday of Advent.

The Order of Readings provides readings for thirty-four Sundays and the weeks following them. In some years, however, there are only thirty-three weeks of Ordinary Time. Further, some Sundays either belong to another season (the Sunday on which the feast of Baptism of the Lord falls and Pentecost) or else are impeded by a solemnity that coincides with Sunday (for example, Holy Trinity or Christ the King).

104. For the correct arrangement in the use of the readings for Ordinary Time, the following are to be respected:

1. The Sunday on which the feast of the Baptism of the Lord falls replaces the first Sunday in Ordinary Time. Therefore the readings of the First Week of Ordinary Time begin

on the Monday after the Sunday following 6 January. When the feast of the Baptism of the Lord is celebrated on Monday because Epiphany has been celebrated on the Sunday, the readings of the First Week begin on Tuesday.

2. The Sunday following the feast of the Baptism of the Lord is the Second Sunday of Ordinary Time. The remaining Sundays are numbered consecutively up to the Sunday preceding the beginning of Lent. The readings for the week in which Ash Wednesday falls are suspended after the Tuesday readings.

3. For the resumption of the readings of Ordinary Time after Pentecost Sunday:

—When there are thirty-four Sundays in Ordinary Time, the week to be used is the one that immediately follows the last week used before Lent.[115]

—When there are thirty-three Sundays in Ordinary Time, the first week that would have been used after Pentecost is omitted, in order to reserve for the end of the year the eschatological texts that are assigned to the last two weeks.[116]

b) Sunday Readings

1) Gospel Readings

105. On the Second Sunday of Ordinary Time the gospel continues to center on the manifestation of the Lord, which Epiphany celebrates through the traditional passage about the wedding feast at Cana and two other passages from John.

Beginning with the Third Sunday, there is a semicontinuous reading of the Synoptic Gospels. This reading is arranged in such a way that as the Lord's life and preaching unfold the teaching proper to each of these Gospels is presented.

This distribution also provides a certain coordination between the meaning of each Gospel and the progress of the liturgical year. Thus after Epiphany the readings are on the beginning of the Lord's preaching and they fit in well with Christ's baptism and the first events in which he manifests himself. The liturgical year leads quite naturally to a termination in the eschatological theme

[115]So, for example, when there are six weeks before Lent, the seventh week begins on the Monday after Pentecost. The solemnity of the Holy Trinity replaces the Sunday of Ordinary Time.

[116]When there are, for example, five weeks before Lent, the Monday after Pentecost begins with the Seventh Week of Ordinary Time and the Sixth Week is dropped.

proper to the last Sundays, since the chapters of the Synoptics that precede the account of the passion treat this eschatological theme rather extensively.

After the Sixteenth Sunday in Year B, five readings are incorporated from John 6 (the discourse on the bread of life). This is the proper place for these readings because the multiplication of the loaves from John takes the place of the same account in Mark. In the semicontinuous reading of Luke for Year C, the introduction of this Gospel has been prefixed to the first text (that is, on the Third Sunday). This passage expresses the author's intention very beautifully and there seemed to be no better place for it.

2) Old Testament readings

106. These readings have been chosen to correspond to the gospel passages in order to avoid an excessive diversity between the readings of different Masses and above all to bring out the unity between the Old and New Testament. The relationship between the readings of the same Mass is shown by a precise choice of the headings prefixed to the individual readings.

To the degree possible, the readings were chosen in such a way that they would be short and easy to grasp. But care has been taken to ensure that many Old Testament texts of major significance would be read on Sundays. Such readings are distributed not according to a logical order but on the basis of what the gospel reading requires. Still, the treasury of the word of God will be opened up in such a way that nearly all the principal pages of the Old Testament will become familiar to those taking part in the Mass on Sunday.

3) Readings from the apostles

107. There is a semicontinuous reading of the Letters of Paul and James. (The Letters of Peter and John are read during the Easter and Christmas seasons.)

Because it is quite long and deals with such diverse issues, the First Letter to the Corinthians has been spread over the three years of the cycle at the beginning of Ordinary Time. It also was thought best to divide Hebrews into two parts; the first part is read in Year B and the second in Year C.

Only readings that are short and readily grasped by the people have been chosen.

Table II at the end of this Introduction[117] indicates the distribution of letters of the apostles over the three-year cycle of the Sundays of Ordinary Time.

---

[117]See Table II at the end of this Introduction.

c) Readings for Solemnities of the Lord During Ordinary Time

108. On the solemnities of Holy Trinity, Corpus Christi, and the Sacred Heart, the texts chosen correspond to the principal themes of these celebrations.

The readings of the Thirty-Fourth and last Sunday of Ordinary Time celebrate Christ the King. He was prefigured by David and heralded as king amid the humiliations of his passion and cross; he reigns in the Church and will come again at the end of time.

d) Weekday Readings

109. 1) The gospels are so arranged that Mark is read first (First to Ninth Week), then Matthew (Tenth to Twenty-first Week), then Luke (Twenty-second to Thirty-fourth Week). Mark 1–12 are read in their entirety, with the exception only of the two passages of Mark 6 that are read on weekdays in other seasons. From Matthew and Luke the readings comprise all the matters not contained in Mark. From all three Synoptics or from two of them, as the case may be, all those passages are read that either are distinctively presented in each Gospel or are needed for a proper understanding of its progression. Jesus' eschatological discourse as contained in its entirety in Luke is read at the end of the liturgical year.

110. 2) The *first reading* is taken in periods of weeks first from the Old then from the New Testament; the number of weeks depends on the length of the biblical books read.

Rather large sections are read from the New Testament books in order to give the substance, as it were, of each of the letters of the apostles.

From the Old Testament there is room only for select passages that, as far as possible, bring out the character of the individual books. The historical texts have been chosen in such a way as to provide an overall view of the history of salvation before the Lord's incarnation. But lengthy narratives could hardly be presented; sometimes verses have been selected that make for a reading of moderate length. In addition, the religious significance of the historical events is sometimes brought out by means of certain texts from the wisdom books that are placed as prologues or conclusions to a series of historical readings.

Nearly all the Old Testament books have found a place in the Order of Readings for weekdays in the Proper of Seasons. The only omissions are the shortest of the prophetic books (Obadiah and Zephaniah) and the poetic book (Song of Solomon). Of those narratives written to edify and requiring a rather long reading to be understood, Tobit and Ruth are included, but Esther and Judith are omitted. (Texts from these two books are assigned to Sundays and weekdays at other times of the year.)

Table III at the end of this Introduction[118] lists the way the books of the Old and the New Testament are distributed over the weekdays in Ordinary Time in the course of two years.

At the end of the liturgical year the readings are from Daniel and Revelation, the books that correspond to the eschatological character of this period.

---

[118]See Table III at the end of this Introduction.

CHAPTER VI

ADAPTATIONS, TRANSLATIONS, AND FORMAT OF THE ORDER OF READINGS

1. ADAPTATIONS AND TRANSLATIONS

111. In the liturgical assembly the word of God must always be read either from the Latin texts prepared by the Holy See or from vernacular translations approved by the conferences of bishops for liturgical use, according to existing norms.[119]

112. The Lectionary for Mass must be translated integrally in all its parts, including the Introduction. If the conference of bishops has judged it necessary and useful to add certain adaptations, these are to be incorporated after their confirmation by the Holy See.[120]

113. The size of the Lectionary will necessitate editions in more than one volume; no particular division of the volumes is prescrib-

---

[119] See Consilium, instruction *De popularibus interpretationibus conficiendis,* 25 Jan. 1969: Notitiae 5 (1969) 3–12; *Declaratio circa interpretationes textuum liturgicorum ad interim paratas:* Notitiae 5 (1969) 69. Congregation for Divine Worship, *Declaratio de interpretatione textuum liturgicorum:* Notitiae 5 (1969) 333–334 (also *Responsiones ad dubia:* Notitiae 9 (1973) 153–154); *De unica interpretatione textuum liturgicorum:* Notitiae 6 (1970) 84–85. Congregation for the Sacraments and Divine Worship, *Epistola ad Praesides Conferentiarum Episcoporum de linguis vulgaribus in S. Liturgiam inducendis:* Notitiae 12 (1976) 300–302.

[120] See Congregation for Divine Worship, instruction *Liturgicae instaurationes,* 5 Sept. 1970, no. 11: AAS 62 (1970) 702–703. General Instruction of the Roman Missal, no. 325.

ed. But each volume is to contain the explanatory texts on the structure and purpose of the section it contains.

The ancient custom is recommended of having separate books, one for the gospels and the other for the readings for the Old and the New Tetstament.

It may also be useful to publish separately a Sunday lectionary, which could also contain selected excerpts from the sanctoral cycle, and a weekday lectionary. A practical basis for dividing the Sunday lectionary is the three-year cycle, so that all the readings for each year are presented in sequence.

But there is freedom to adopt other arrrangements that may be devised and seem to have pastoral advantages.

114. The texts for the chants are always to be adjoined to the readings, but separate books containing the chants alone are permitted. It is recommended that the texts be printed with divisions into stanzas.

115. Whenever a text consists of different parts, the typography must make this structure of the text clear. It is likewise recommended that even nonpoetic texts be printed with division into sense lines to assist the proclamation of the readings.

116. Where there are long and short forms of a text, they are to be printed separately so that each can be read with ease. But if such a separation does not seem feasible, a way is to be found to ensure that each text can be proclaimed without mistakes.

117. In vernacular editions the texts are not be to printed without the headings prefixed. If it seems advisable, an introductory note on the general meaning of the passage may be added to the heading. This note is to carry some distinctive symbol or is to be set in different type to show clearly that it is an optional text.[121]

118. It would be useful for every volume to have an index of the passages of the Bible, modeled on the biblical index of the present volume.[122] This will provide ready access to texts of the lectionaries for Mass that may be needed or helpful for specific occasions.

2. FORMAT OF INDIVIDUAL READINGS

For each reading the present volume carries the textual reference, the heading, and the *incipit*.

a) Text References

119. The text reference (that is, chapter and verse) is always given

---

[121] See General Instruction of the Roman Missal, nos. 11, 29, 68a, 139.

[122] See Index of Readings at the end of the Lectionary.

according to the Neo-Vulgate edition, except for the psalms.[123] But a second reference according to the original text (Hebrew, Aramaic, or Greek) has been added wherever there is a discrepancy. Depending on the decrees of the competent authorities for the individual languages, vernacular versions may retain the enumeration corresponding to the version of the Bible approved for liturgical use by the same authorities. Exact references to chapter and verses, however, must always appear and may be given in the text or in the margin.

120. These references provide liturgical books with the source of the "announcement" *(inscriptio)* of the text that must be read in the celebration, but which is not printed in this volume. This "announcement" of the text will observe the following norms, but they may be altered by decree of the competent authorities on the basis of what is customary and useful for different places and languages.

121. 1) The formula to be used is always: "A *reading* from the Book of . . . ," "A *reading* from the Letter of . . . ," or "A *reading* from the Gospel of . . . ," and not: "The *beginning* of . . ." (unless this seems advisable in particular instances) or: "*Continuation* of . . ."

122. 2) The traditionally accepted titles for books are to be retained, with the following exceptions:

    a. Where there are two books with the same name, the title is to be: The First Book, The Second Book (e.g., of Kings, of Maccabees) or The First Letter, The Second Letter.

    b. The title more common in current usage is to be accepted for the following books:
       I and II Samuel instead of I and II Kings;
       I and II Kings instead of III and IV Kings;
       I and II Chronicles instead of I and II Paralipomenon;
       Books of Ezra and Nehemiah instead of I and II Ezra.

    c. The distinguishing titles for the wisdom books are: Book of Job, Book of Proverbs, Book of Ecclesiastes or Qoheleth, Song of Songs, Book of Wisdom, Book of Ecclesiasticus or Sirach.

    d. For all the books that are included among the prophets in the Neo-Vulgate, the formula is to be: "A reading from the Book of Isaiah, or of Jeremiah or of Baruch" and: "A read-

---

[123] The references for the psalms follow the order of the *Liber Psalmorum*, published by the Pontifical Commission for the Neo-Vulgate (Vatican Polyglot Press, 1969).

ing from the Prophecy of Ezekiel, of Daniel, of Hosea, of
Malchi," even in the case of books not universally regarded as in fact prophetic.

e. The title is to be Book of Lamentations and Letter to the Hebrews, with no mention of Jeremiah and Paul.

b) Heading

123. There is a *heading* prefixed to each text, chosen carefully
(usually from the words of the text itself) in order to point out the
main theme of the reading and, when necessary, to make the connection between the readings of the same Mass clear.

c) Incipit

124. In this Order of Readings the first element of the *incipit* is the
customary introductory phrase, "At the time," "In those days,"
"Brothers and Sisters," "Dearly Beloved." or "Thus says the
Lord." These words are not given when the text itself provides suf-

TABLE I
Seasonal Table of Principal Celebrations of the Liturgical Yea

Year	Sunday Cycle	Weekday Cycle	Ash Wednesday	Easter	Ascension	Pent
1981	A	I	4 March	19 April	28 May	7
1982	B	II	24 Feb.	11 April	20 May	30
1983	C	I	16 Feb.	3 April	12 May	22
1984	A	II	7 March	22 April	31 May	10
1985	B	I	20 Feb.	7 April	16 May	26
1986	C	II	12 Feb.	30 March	8 May	18
1987	A	I	4 March	19 April	28 May	7
1988	B	II	17 Feb.	3 April	12 May	22
1989	C	I	8 Feb.	26 March	4 May	14
1990	A	II	28 Feb.	15 April	24 May	3
1991	B	I	13 Feb.	31 March	9 May	19
1992	C	II	4 March	19 April	28 May	7
1993	A	I	24 Feb.	11 April	20 May	30
1994	B	II	16 Feb.	3 April	12 May	22
1995	C	I	1 March	16 April	25 May	4
1996	A	II	21 Feb.	7 April	16 May	26
1997	B	I	12 Feb.	30 March	8 May	18
1998	C	II	25 Feb.	12 April	21 May	31
1999	A	I	17 Feb.	4 April	13 May	23
2000	B	II	8 March	23 April	1 June	11

ficient indication of the time or the persons involved or where such phrases would not fit in with the very nature of the text. For the individual languages, such phrases may be changed or dropped by decree of the competent authorities.

After the first words of the *incipit* the Order of Readings gives the proper *beginning of the reading,* with some words deleted or supplied for intelligibility, inasmuch as the text is separated from its context. When the text for a reading is made up of nonconsecutive verses and this has required changes in wording, these are appropriately indicated.

d) Final Acclamation

125. In order to facilitate the congregation's acclamation, the words for the reader *This is the word of the Lord,* or similar words suited to local custom, are to be printed at the end of the reading for use by the reader.

Weeks of Ordinary Time				First Sunday of Advent
before Lent		after Easter season		
ending	in week no.	beginning	in week no.	
3 March	8	8 June	10	29 Nov.
23 Feb.	7	31 May	9	28 Nov.
15 Feb.	6	23 May	8	27 Nov.
6 March	9	11 June	10	2 Dec.
19 Feb.	6	27 May	8	1 Dec.
11 Feb.	5	19 May	7	30 Nov.
3 March	8	8 June	10	29 Nov.
16 Feb.	6	23 May	8	27 Nov.
7 Feb.	5	15 May	6	3 Dec.
27 Feb.	8	4 June	9	2 Dec.
12 Feb.	5	20 May	7	1 Dec.
3 March	8	8 June	10	29 Nov.
23 Feb.	7	31 May	9	28 Nov.
15 Feb.	6	23 May	8	27 Nov.
28 Feb.	8	5 June	9	3 Dec.
20 Feb.	7	27 May	8	1 Dec.
11 Feb.	5	19 May	7	30 Nov.
24 Feb.	7	1 June	9	29 Nov.
16 Feb.	6	24 May	8	28 Nov.
7 March	9	12 June	10	3 Dec.

TABLE II

Arrangement of the Second Reading on the Sundays of Ordinary Time

Sunday	Year A	Year B	Year C
2	1 Corinthians 1–4	1 Corinthians 6–11	1 Corinthians 12–15
3	,,	,,	,,
4	,,	,,	,,
5	,,	,,	,,
6	,,	,,	,,
7	,,	2 Corinthians	,,
8	,,	,,	,,
9	Romans	,,	Galatians
10	,,	,,	,,
11	,,	,,	,,
12	,,	,,	,,
13	,,	,,	,,
14	,,	,,	,,
15	,,	Ephesians	Colossians
16	,,	,,	,,
17	,,	,,	,,
18	,,	,,	,,
19	,,	,,	Hebrews 11–12
20	,,	,,	,,
21	,,	,,	,,
22	,,	James	,,
23	,,	,,	Philemon
24	,,	,,	1 Timothy
25	Philippians	,,	,,
26	,,	,,	,,
27	,,	Hebrews 2–10	2 Timothy
28	,,	,,	,,
29	1 Thessalonians	,,	,,
30	,,	,,	,,
31	,,	,,	2 Thessalonians
32	,,	,,	,,
33	,,	,,	,,

TABLE III

Arrangement of the First Reading on the Weekdays of Ordinary Time

Week	Year I	Year II
1	Hebrews	1 Samuel
2	,,	,,
3	,,	2 Samuel
4	,,	2 Samuel; 1 Kings 1–16
5	Genesis 1–11	1 Kings 1–16
6	,,	James
7	Sirach (Ecclesiasticus)	,,
8	,,	1 Peter; Jude
9	Tobit	2 Peter; 2 Timothy
10	2 Corinthians	1 Kings 17–22
11	,,	1 Kings 17–22; 2 Kings
12	Genesis 12–50	2 Kings; Lamentations
13	,,	Amos
14	,,	Hosea; Isaiah
15	Exodus	Isaiah; Micah
16	,,	Micah; Jeremiah
17	Exodus; Leviticus	Jeremiah
18	Numbers; Deuteronomy	Jeremiah; Nahum; Habakkuk
19	Deuteronomy; Joshua	Ezekiel
20	Judges; Ruth	,,
21	1 Thessalonians	2 Thessalonians; 1 Corinthians
22	1 Thessalonians; Colossians	1 Corinthians
23	Colossians; 1 Timothy	,,
24	1 Timothy	,,
25	Ezra; Haggai; Zechariah	Proverbs; Qoheleth (Ecclesiastes)
26	Zechariah; Nehemiah; Baruch	Job
27	Jonah; Malachi; Joel	Galatians
28	Romans	Galatians; Ephesians
29	,,	Ephesians
30	,,	,,
31	,,	Ephesians; Philippians
32	Wisdom	Titus, Philemon; 2 and 3 John
33	1 and 2 Maccabees	Revelation
34	Daniel	,,

To Hear and Proclaim

by Ralph A. Keifer

Preface

The publication of the new Introduction to the lectionary marks a significant turn in official liturgical documents. It deserves a warm welcome and careful study. It is positive about new developments among the churches of the Roman rite, effectively canonizing those developments by acknowledging them in the official introduction to our most important liturgical book. The Introduction reflects a refreshing return to that urbane *Romanita* which, while cautious over theory and respectful of precedent, quietly permits the new to grow where the old has been found wanting. A document that addresses everything from lay preaching to the use of leaflet missals, while condemning nothing, accepting much, and reproving little, represents a landmark in official commentary on liturgical practice. The Introduction is Roman, Catholic, collegial, and official. Like all of those things, it is not perfect. But here is a document with which the churches of God can breathe and grow. It is a happy affirmation of the Petrine ministry among the churches.

I have carefully avoided a line by line commentary. This would do violence to the urbane spirit of the document as well as to the sensibilities of the reader. What is obvious needs no commentary, and much of what the document says speaks clearly for itself. But before all else, this is a pastoral, not a legalistic document. It would be ungratefully contrary to its spirit to attempt to interpret it as if it were a set of recipes. I have therefore sought mainly to underline its fundamental principles, especially in those areas where those principles seem to be least understood and, therefore, most often neglected.

I have especially underlined the question of the relation of Christian initiation to eucharistic celebration and the vexing problem of our still unreformed interpretation of the introductory rites of the mass. I did so because the renewal of liturgical life is (as the Introduction asserts in a variety of ways) integrally and organically related to the question of the development of a Catholic lay consciousness of mission in the world as a consecrated people. We can only come into our own as hearers of the word by patterns of initiation and celebration which affirm that baptismal spirituality.

This book is designed especially (though not exclusively) for those who have a pastoral ministry, including, especially, musicians. I will disappoint those who are looking for recipes. This is only to respect the role of the practitioner. What the pastoral minister can best take from us "theoreticians" is a reflective horizon for their own tasks. Now, more than ever, we need that reflective horizon.

My section of the commentary is gratefully dedicated to the St. Giles Family Mass Community of Chicago, who struggle so valiantly to live their mission as an assembly of the faithful, and especially to Kathleen Sullivan-Stewart, who so relentlessly challenges me on the issues I raise here.

I wish to acknowledge my gratitude to the Crosier Community of Ft. Wayne, Indiana, especially Fr. Robert Zahrt, for their hospitality while this manuscript was being prepared. Also, my thanks goes to Virgil Funk, Daniel Connors, Michelle Dunkle and everyone at NPM who helped this book come to fruition.

1
The Reform Continues

Nearly a generation after Vatican II, we are still grappling with the fulfillment of the Council's ideal of a liturgy reformed and renewed, a truly popular liturgy in which all participate to the full. For better or worse, we are living in a time of liturgical experiment. Now by "experiment" I do not necessarily mean that people are doing strange things in secret chapels. I mean what the word normally means, that we are doing things we have not done before, and we are doing them with no certainty of their outcome. In that process, we are discovering that some things work well, and some do not. As the experiment goes on, we are discovering that we have made some false starts, and that there are some basic principles to which we need to return again and again. As with all experiments, we are finding that, in a number of cases, we may have started off less than well informed. And, as with all good experiments, we often find that the tried and true is a block to moving ahead in ways that could be more creative and liberating, and indeed, more faithful to the spirit of the reform.

In view of this situation, the appearance of a new Introduction to the lectionary could not come at a more welcome time. The Introduction carefully situates the lectionary within the context of the liturgical event of the liturgy of the word. It calls us to a serious reconsideration of what the reform of the liturgy of the word was about, and it calls us to be reflective about what we have done to implement that reform. And here, in the liturgy of the word, is the most fertile field of liturgical experimentation. The reform presented us with a pattern without parallel in recent Catholic experience. Also—something Catholics in this country seem to be unaware of—the Catholic liturgy of the word represents a very different form of religious expression than does the ordinary Protestant Sunday service of praise, prayer, and preaching. Those Protestant services took their original pattern more from the Divine Office (or Liturgy of the Hours) of the medieval church than from its eucharistic liturgy. The too-ready borrowing of forms from this tradition (whether of hymnody or of preaching) may only have compounded our difficulties rather than solved them.

The very notion of a "liturgy of the word" was new to most Catholics less than a generation ago. The reminiscences of this writer may serve to jog the memories of others as ancient as himself. A convert less to the "old church" than to a hope of a Catholicism renewed, I had become something of a devotee of the movement for liturgical renewal in the late fifties and early sixties. I had cut my Catholic teeth on one of its chief publications, *Orate Fratres* (now *Worship*), and, in college and graduate school, had become one of a rising army of young advocates of liturgical reform. Yet my first experience of the "new mass" late in the fall of 1964, the hybridized part-Latin, part-English mass, gave me something of a shock.

It was not the use of congregational responses or the singing of hymns or the introduction of the English language that shocked me. These I had taken for granted as a Protestant child, and had been scandalized by their absence in Catholic worship. Moreover, I had had a taste of all these things at mass in college, in a religious community, and in graduate school. With a little creativity, it was possible to disguise the old Latin mass under song, commentary, and people's prayers in English, in such a way as to make it "feel" like a vernacular and participatory liturgy. They were doing this very successfully in a small chapel on the campus where I was a graduate student. If anything, the official and parish version of what I had already experienced struck me in many ways as inferior. At the campus masses the year before, the music had been richer and more sensitively employed, the ceremony simpler, the vernacular used more fully, and participation both easier and more enthusiastic.

If I felt gratified by the triumph of a cause I had taken up years before, I was also disappointed by its first practical results in my parish church. But when I say I experienced shock, this is not the kind of shock I mean. I refer to the shock of the experience of the unfolding of the first half of the mass rite *away from the altar*. This was not something I had counted on. In the old liturgy, even at its solemn best, the liturgy of the word functioned simply as an ornate prelude to the "real" liturgical event, the liturgy of the eucharist. Everything in my Catholic experience had taught me to perceive it that way. The very names of the two parts of the mass then commonly in use—"mass of the catechumens" (liturgy of the word), and "mass of the faithful" (liturgy of the eucharist)—suggested that the first part was merely prelude. Because the more frequent experience of mass was low mass, with the priest remaining at the altar for the whole liturgy of the word (with only himself reading), the ritual reinforced the perception that the liturgy of the word was a prelude to the key altar-event of liturgy of the eucharist. The reading of scripture translations in the vernacular and the sermon itself were treated (in fact, though not in church legislation) as options at the discretion of the celebrant. Frequently, preaching occurred *after* the mass, and no priest felt obliged, as they do now, to preach at every single Sunday eucharist.

Likewise, the catechism spoke of the three *principal* parts of the mass as "offertory, consecration, and communion," with the strong suggestion that whatever the "mass of the catechumens" was, it was not "principal." And it was common teaching that while it was a grave obligation to attend mass on Sunday, the grave obligation extended only to the "principal parts." By separating the liturgy of the word from the altar, and by describing the mass as divided into two principal parts—liturgy of the word and liturgy of the eucharist—Pope Paul VI and the other agents of the Vatican II liturgical reforms were asserting the importance of the liturgy of the word in its own right, not as prelude to the liturgy of the eucharist, but as integrally related to it.

It was this that shocked me about the new mass, not the shock of dismay, but the shock of surprise. Here was a liturgical pattern utterly new to my experience. What struck me most was not the introduction of a lectern facing the people (this only made good practical sense if you are going to read a text in the vernacular), but the introduction of lay readers, the seating of the priest during the lessons and his standing *away* from the altar for dialogue and prayer. On reflection, what surprised me was that it recast the liturgy of the word as the action of a deliberative assembly (its secular analogue being, for example, the formal meeting of the Senate), placing the priest not only as minister but also as hearer, and at the same time, placing the people not only as hearers but as active agents of the liturgy. It made the liturgy of the word, as the General Instruction of the Roman Missal was later to say, "an action of the entire church hierarchically assembled."

And so this is why I begin with a reminiscence of the beginnings of liturgical reform. That reform has not been carried out fully. We still do not experience the liturgy of the word as an action of the whole assembly. The publication of a new Introduction to the lectionary offers an occasion to ask ourselves some questions about how we might both grasp more deeply the intentions of Pope Paul VI and the other reformers, and carry that reform out more fully.

Perhaps the thing we still have to get into our heads—and into our patterns of prayer and celebration—is the definition of the liturgy of the word as a *liturgy*. That is easier said than done. In many ways, the pre-Vatican II perception of the liturgy of the word as a prelude to the main event is a perception that remains firmly in place. Only now, instead of its being understood as a ritual prelude, it is understood as a didactic prelude. How often is one of the most significant opening statements of the presider, "The theme of today's mass is . . . "? How often do the invitations to the prayer of the faithful (general intercessions) sound like reminiscences of points made in the day's reading or homily? Or how often does somebody assigned the task of preparing the intercessions assume that her task is to provide an echo of the day's "theme"? In looking for the right music, how often does the responsible musician strain to find a coherent "theme" that binds the three readings together—just as the conscientious preacher does in preparing the homily? How often do we hear in preaching workshops, "But how will we *get* them (meaning, of course, *instruct* them) unless we get them with the homily?" All of these efforts and concerns reflect an assumption that the major and virtually exclusive purpose of the liturgy of the word is didactic—to make some point that can be duly noted and taken home, a distinctive "message for the day," distilled into a "theme," announced at the beginning of mass, elaborated in song and prayer, and made the focus of the day's homily.

This mania for theme, which has overtaken virtually all planning and preaching, does not reflect a renewed appreciation of a reformed liturgy of the word. Rather, it reflects a failure to understand the reformed liturgy of the word at all. The preoccupation with "theme" did indeed come in the wake of Vatican II, but it is derived more from a residue of pre-reform assumptions and practices than it is from Vatican II's principles of liturgical reform and renewal.

Before Vatican II, preaching and the liturgy of the word (such as it was) had only a tenuous connection with one another. There was no embarrassment in not "preaching from the readings." If the celebrant chose to preach at all, it was on any topic of his, the pastor's, or the bishop's choice. I can personally remember a sermon on the seven dolors of the Blessed Virgin on Pentecost day.

Normally, preaching fell into three basic types (with certain other variants for retreats and missions)—devotional fervorinos, moral exhortations, and doctrinal instructions. The devotional fervorino aimed at a deeper appreciation of and prayerful response to some saint, or to the Virgin, or to the Lord Jesus Christ, or to some aspect of the Christian mystery (e.g., the passion of Christ, God's love manifest in the Sacred Heart, or Christ's presence in the eucharist). More affective ("emotional") than intellectual, this sort of preaching was aimed at swaying the emotions toward prayer and devotion.

The moral exhortation shared certain similarities of style with the devotional fervorino, but it took as its topical point some proposed behavior (or proposed avoidance of behavior) and attempted to move the hearers to respond as the church would want them to. The moral exhortation might well involve an exposition of the church's teaching on a given point, but its aim and tone were also more affective than didactic: the concern was to move to action rather than simply to inform.

The doctrinal exposition aimed at just that—exposing the teaching of the church for the reflection and understanding of the hearers. It might end in exhortation to one sort of behavior or another, but its main purpose was informative. However much its content might at times be accommodated to simple audiences, the content remained fundamentally intellectual—the hearer was expected to be moved to understanding, to come away from the event better instructed.

This sort of preaching rested on a whole fabric of practice and perspective that was seriously disrupted in the wake of Vatican II. Almost overnight, the older devotional patterns dropped out of use, sometimes abandoned enthusiastically, sometimes with regret, but in any case, almost everywhere in this country, abandoned. Equally important, the agreed consensus on how matters of faith and morals should be approached was disturbed by a variety of factors. The handbook that prepared and sustained generations of preachers was the Catechism of the Council of Trent, complete with examples and sermon hints of all sorts. But the Council of Trent had been called to combat the crisis of the Reformation, while Vatican II was called to bring healing to the wounds of division among Christians. The Catechism of the Council of Trent, measured against the documents of Vatican II, began to appear not only dangerously quaint, but also appallingly anti-Protestant and drearily unecumenical. The Catechism also cast its teaching in the mold of scholastic categories—categories which Vatican II generally abandoned for its own teachings, and which were being abandoned in theology generally. To complicate the situation further, a revolution in Catholic ethical thinking also occurred just after Vatican II. While especially explosive issues (like that of birth control) attracted more attention in the news media, there was a general shift away from the legalistic and ritualistic ethics of the "old church"—a shift that occurred at all levels from academic theology to popular perceptions. In a word, all the formerly taken for granted points of reference for preaching either shifted dramatically or disappeared entirely.

At the same moment that this was occurring, we began to use a vernacular liturgy that was cast in a somewhat sparse and stark language style (especially when compared with previous familiar devotional language) and wedded to a ritual that was (compared to that of the past) equally sparse and stark. "Simplicity" became the hallmark of liturgical reform. All of this, together with a surge of enthusiasm for the idea of "full, conscious, and active" participation of the people, conspired to give the whole new liturgical enterprise a decidedly didactic cast. The protest against the more ornate and obscure ceremonial of the past never quite reached the fever pitch of the reformation criticism of "dark and dumb ceremonies." Still, the "new liturgy" was generally introduced under the rubric of intelligibility. Understanding and clarity were everything.

As the old landmarks for preaching disappeared, and the "new liturgy" was introduced with the apologetic that people would "understand" better, the new directives also appeared and directed the priest to (a) preach "from the readings"; and (b) to do so at least on all Sundays and feast days. The best the average preacher could salvage from his own training and the new directives was the notion that the homily was to be an instruction on the readings, and the best that liturgical planners could do was to conclude that the liturgy of the word was simply a pattern for instructing the people. Such conclusions may have been unfortunate, but, given the climate of the time, they are understandable.

Without denying that instruction has a place in the liturgy of the word, it must be insisted that "instruction" must be rightly understood, and that, in any case, "instruction" is not the only, and perhaps not the primary function of the liturgy of the word. All too often, under the influence of the conditions that prevailed when the "new liturgy" was introduced, "instruction" has meant, in effect, the imparting of ideas about the content of the Catholic and Christian faith, or the giving of information about living it. Integral as these things may be to the proclamation and celebration of the word, they scarcely exhaust it. The mania for "theme," which so preoccupies preachers and planners, is generally alien to both the forms and spirit of the Roman liturgy, because it is based on a much too didactic understanding of the liturgy of the word and of the meaning of "instruction."

If, then, the function of the liturgy of the word is more than to "instruct" on a theme, what is that function? The function of the liturgy of the word, as the Introduction to the lectionary presupposes, is to *celebrate the mystery of Christ's presence among us.* The heart of the first chapter of the Introduction is No. 3:

> The many riches contained in the one word of God are admirably brought out in the different kinds of liturgical celebrations and liturgical assemblies. This takes place as the unfolding mystery of Christ is recalled during the course of the liturgical year, as the Church's sacraments and sacramentals are celebrated, or as the faithful respond individually to the Holy Spirit working within them. For then the liturgical celebration, based primarily on the word of God and sustained by it, becomes a new event and enriches the word itself with new meaning and power. Thus in the liturgy the Church faithfully adheres to the way Christ himself read and explained the Scriptures, beginning with the "today" of his coming forward in the synagogue and urging all to search the Scriptures.

The rich density of these lines deserves further probing, and we would not do the Introduction justice unless we paused over them. The appeal to "the way Christ himself read and explained the Scriptures, beginning with the 'today' of his coming forward in the synagogue and urging all to search the Scriptures," is the key to the proper understanding of No. 3. The footnote of the text refers the reader to the fourth chapter of the Gospel according to Luke, where Jesus comes forward in the synagogue to read the lesson:

> He came to Nazareth where he had been reared, and entering the synagogue on the sabbath as he was in the habit of doing, he stood up to do the reading. When the book of the prophet Isaiah was handed him, he unrolled the scroll and found the passage where it was written:
>
> > "The spirit of the Lord is upon me;
> > therefore he has anointed me.
> > He has sent me to being glad tidings
> > to the poor,
> > to proclaim liberty to captives,

> Recovery of sight to the blind
> and release to prisoners,
> To announce a year of favor from
> the Lord."
>
> Rolling up the scroll he gave it back to the assistant and sat down. All in the synagogue had their eyes fixed on him. Then he began by saying to them, "Today this Scripture passage is fulfilled in your hearing."

The biblical text read by Jesus calls the hearers to ponder, not some event in past time, but One present in their midst. As portrayed by St. Luke, Jesus takes the text of Isaiah's promise and points to himself (though not to himself alone, but also to his work among those he touched in the Israel of God). The text functions not as handing on something from time past as much as it does as a pointer to what God is doing here and now. The proclamation occurs, not in the bald reading of the text, nor in commentary about what God may have done in time past, but in the moment when text and preacher name what God is doing here and now, and challenge those present to a response. The proclamation of the word (reading and preaching) serves not simply to inform, but rather to reveal, to call attention to the event of God in the world. Rather than interpreting the text, the proclamation takes the text to interpret *the assembly of hearers*: it tells them how God is acting in their midst.

Within the context of the liturgy, this will only be appreciated to the extent that we are also able to appreciate that the liturgical assembly itself is a real presence of Christ (see Chapter II, No. 7 of the General Instruction of the Roman Missal). This, indeed, is the proper function of entrance rites—to call the assembly to an awareness of that presence of Christ in its midst. It is most unfortunate that we have chosen to concentrate on entrance hymns experienced as welcomes of the celebrant or as didactic prologues celebrating today's "theme," rather than following the directions of the sacramentary and learning to highlight the *Kyrie* (Lord, have mercy) litany and the *Gloria* anthem as exuberant acclamatory welcomes of the Lord who is present in our midst to heal and to save (see Nos. 30 and 31 of the General Instruction of the Roman Missal). Yet this is more than a simple question of musical selection or liturgical planning. In its conception of the proclamation of the word, the Introduction is calling us to a task that is in many ways barely begun: the recovery of the spirituality of the praying assembly, the restoration of the assembly's sense that it is Christ the Lord who is present by the very fact of the baptized having gathered together.

The ancient Syrian *Didascalia Apostolorum,* a document on the ordering of church life from the latter part of the third century, contains an interesting exhortation to regular attendance at the Sunday liturgy. It exhorts people to be present "lest the body of Christ lack a member." What sense of responsibility toward one another, what sense of one another's dignity as the anointed of God must that community have had! How many contemporary parishes could exhort the ordinary worshiper (credibly, that is): "Please come, you'll be missed; please come, your part is vital to what we are doing; please come, your presence makes a difference." A well-known priest writes for a presumably well-informed audience of lay Catholics that he celebrates Christmas mass in Latin America every year so that "people who would not otherwise have Christ's presence will have it then." While it is possible to admire the devotion to ministry and the eucharistic piety in this statement, it is also possible to wonder if a generation of liturgical renewal has made any difference at all to the ordinary believer's perceptions (whether that ordinary believer be priest or lay person) of the nature of the liturgical assembly.

That the liturgical assembly actually "represents Christ" because that assembly itself is indeed a mode of Christ's presence, is a truth that remains largely lost to piety and perception. How little we have learned to treasure a sense of Christ present in the assembly is doubtless manifest in our conventional patterns of church renovation. As most parish churches are laid out, the worshiper in the pew is spatially, kinesthetically, and visually related only to the sanctuary. Our placement of the people leaves them (in relation to one another) as solitary "attenders" of an action which takes place in the sanctuary. Nothing in the architecture suggests that the people have a relationship to one another beyond sharing a common role as spectators. Most church renovations fail to remedy this at all: again and again renovation means sanctuary renovation, the people's space being left exactly as it was before Vatican II. The same may be said of pious practices. If we had any sort of lively appreciation of the presence of Christ in the assembly, we would be incapable of the Holy Week passion reading travesty of assigning the assembly of the people the voices of those who called for Christ's death (an assignment made by inept leaflets and missalettes, not by the official liturgical books).

In a variety of ways, the Introduction to the lectionary is careful to touch upon the many facets of the renewal of church life that are needed if the renewed celebration of the word is to have its full effect. It is significant that the Introduction does not speak only of the celebration of the word at mass. Rather, it speaks of that celebration taking place "as the unfolding mystery of Christ is recalled during the course of the liturgical year, as the church's sacraments and sacramentals are celebrated, or as the faithful respond individually to the Holy Spirit working within them" (No. 3). By this appeal to other contexts of the celebration of the word, and by its implicit insistence that the proclamation of the word serves to reveal the event of God in the world, the Introduction, by implication, situates the renewal of the eucharistic liturgy of the word and the renewal of preaching within the wider context of the renewal of church life, and especially of the renewal of Christian initiation. We might add—for reasons to be explained shortly—that the renewal of the practice of the sacrament of reconciliation is implied as well. For the assembly's consciousness of itself as embodying Christ's presence will doubtless depend much upon how deeply people have appropriated a sense of being truly "christened"—anointed as God's holy ones, commissioned as agents of the kingdom of God in the world, enfranchised as responsible participants in the life of the city of God in the world. It is Christian initiation that constitutes people as members of the Christian assembly, Christian initiation that buries them with Christ and anoints them with his Spirit to stand with the assembly of the faithful to offer the world to God. It is Christian initiation, in other words, that constitutes the assembly as "representing Christ."

The sacramental bases of Christ's presence in the assembly are the sacraments of initiation. If baptism is seen only as rescue from original sin, confirmation as graduation from catechetics, and first eucharist as a cute and cuddly domestic event, we lose the cutting edge of these sacraments as enfranchising people for active participation in the liturgy and active mission in the world. In other words, if the liturgical assembly is to have a lively sense of itself having Christ present in its midst, it will need the recurring experience of the full initiation of adults in its midst. Just as the premier experience of the New Testament is Christ's resurrection from the dead, so the central liturgical experience is the rising of new Christians from the font into the life of the Spirit. To the extent that this experience animates liturgical celebration, to that same extent the assembly will have a grasp of itself as the locale of Christ's living presence. The public process of the making of adult Christians is designed both for the new Christian and also for the benefit of the already baptized. The point of "putting the candidates through" the various public steps of initiation—from their enrollment as catechumens all the way to the mystagogy of their first Easter season as baptized people—is to give a public demonstration of what it means that God works in the world in the lives of ordinary people.

Also, in a world where church attendance is more and more voluntary, rather than compelled by social pressure, some thought might well be given to developing public processes whereby people who have been away are formally reconciled to the church. This is not to suggest a restoration of "public penance," if that is understood as a public humiliation of the wayward. Rather, it is to suggest that we need a process whereby people can rediscover a home in the midst of the believing community, and where, at the same time, those who have not left are called to a deeper appreciation of what it means to be the assembly of the faithful. Most people, after all, do not "leave the church" to live a life of sin and degradation. As most of us are aware, it does not require leaving the church to live such a life. There are plenty of people who are able to combine sinning and churchgoing.

Most people who leave do so, in fact, because they have been sinned against. They leave wounded or scandalized in some way, often in many ways. Their return reflects a recovery of a sense of Christ's presence in the church, a renewed appreciation of a human church where God has chosen to dwell. The process of reconciliation to the church has, in many ways, as much to do with the returnee forgiving the church as with the church forgiving the returnee. It is access to this graced process which the assembly of the faithful needs and deserves. A public process of reconciliation for those returning to the church could have almost as potent an effect on the renewal of church life as does the implementation of the Rite of the Christian Initiation of Adults.

As those who work with the Rite of the Christian Initiation of Adults soon discover, a serious effort at the renewal of Christian initiation (as would also be the case with a serious effort at the renewal of reconciliation) involves much more than the implementation of another program in the parish. The new materials on Christian Initiation ultimately call for a renewal of parish life and ministry, and with it, the renewal of parish structures. If the church is to be faithful to its own Catholicity, that renewal is a practical necessity, not a visionary dream. Catholicism is a sacramental religion. This means, among other things, that it believes that its very patterns of life and worship are themselves points of meeting between God and God's people. In the final analysis, what Catholic Christianity is about is the mystery of God present among God's people (including the structures of church life, worship, and ministry). Because of this, fidelity to the Catholic understanding of Christianity requires constant attention to the patterns of life and worship that best lead people to those points of meeting, and that best help people to appreciate these points as manifestations of God's grace. The kind of Catholicism that we Americans developed in response to the immigrant situation, with its professional few ministering to a large and amorphous many, leaves us constantly open to the danger of making the church look (and act) like a spiritual bureaucracy. The amorphous and rather passive worshiping assembly of conventional Catholicism (which is a fairly accurate mirror of the actual functioning of the parish) is scarcely a clear pointer to the meeting between God and his people, scarcely a vibrant witness to that presence of Christ in the assembly which is so heavily underscored by the official documents.

The understanding of church and liturgy found in all the official documents on liturgical celebration demands that, on every level of church life, both within the liturgy and outside it, we reconsider the model of the professional few ministering to the anonymous many, which dominates most parish life today. Instead of parishes with three or six or ten masses on Sunday, we need parishes that have regrouped themselves so that they are parishes of three or six or ten communities of faith where people minister to one another and where people are sustained and sent out to their mission in the world. The present crisis of ministry—with the growing shortage of priests and even more dramatically declining numbers of the religious sisters who formerly carried so much of the church's ministry—is a crisis that carries the real danger of beauracratizing the church even more, with the few priests we have left becoming the chairmen of boards of professional lay ministers. This may be efficient, but we need to ask seriously whether this is fully Catholic and sacramental. In view of the way the official documents accord a sacred character to the assembly of all the faithful, the kinds of new ministries and patterns of church life that seem most in need of cherishing are those that are less formal, less professionalized, and more apt to foster a sense of Christ's presence among all the people of God.

To speak, then, of the renewal of Christian initiation, and, by implication, of the renewal of reconciliation, is not to speak simply of the addition of some new program. It is to speak of a renewal of the church's structure, its patterns of life and ministry. One of the most vexing problems of church life is the felt disconnection between life and liturgy. Yet if they seem to have so little to do with one another, it is because they have lost their anchor in initiation and reconciliation. Only an assembly that knows what it means to rise to new life can celebrate it; only an assembly that

has felt the breath of the Spirit alive in the world can give thanks
for the work of God in history; only an assembly that has sensed
the action of God in its midst can make sense of a scripture that
proclaims a Lord of history. This is underscored in Nos. 6 and 7 of
the Introduction: it is from the perspective of an anticipated
renewal of initiation and reconciliation that these two critical sections (The Word of God in the Liturgical Participation of the
Faithful and The Word of God in the Church's Life) make the most
sense. The Introduction assumes an integral connection between
liturgy and life: "In celebrating the liturgy, the Church faithfully
echoes the Amen that Christ, the mediator between God and
humanity, uttered once for all as he shed his blood to seal God's
new covenant in the Holy Spirit" (No. 6). Authentic liturgical participation is not simply a matter of "devout attendance," but is,
rather, a matter of committing one's life to Christ: ". . . the
faithful's participation in the liturgy increases to the degree that as
they listen to the word of God spoken in the liturgy they strive
harder to commit themselves to the Word of God made flesh in
Christ" (No. 6). In No. 7, the grounding of the celebration of the
word in the experience of Christian initiation is made explicit. The
"remembrance of the Lord" (Do this in memory of me), which is at
the heart of liturgical prayer, is not simply a remembrance of what
God has done in the remote past. It is the remembrance of the living church's experience of the Lord, a renewal of the covenant
made in baptism and confirmation:

"Whenever, therefore, the Church, gathered by the Holy
Spirit for liturgical celebration, announces and proclaims the word of God, it has the experience of being a
new people in whom the covenant made in the past is
fulfilled. Baptism and confirmation in the Spirit have
made all the faithful messengers of God's word . . ."
(No. 7).

The Introduction's understanding that the word of God is the
word of Christ present in the assembly is grounded in its perception of the word as *sacramental.* This is not to suggest that the proclamation of the word constitutes some sort of "eighth
sacrament." Rather, the word is sacramental as the church is
sacramental. When we say that the church is "sacramental" we do
not simply mean that it is an organization that has a set of rites
called sacraments. The church is more than simply a dispenser of
sacraments. Rather, when we say that the church is "sacramental"
we mean that the church itself is a "sacrament"—that the church
is, in a real sense, the presence of God in the world. God is present
in the world in and through his people, including his people's way

of life, and their shaping of life together—including, indeed, as part of that way of life and that shaping of life together, those particular actions we call sacraments. This is indeed a mystery, for that presence of God in and through his people is marked and shaped by the course of human history as it is marred and defaced by the tragedy of human sinfulness. One of the perennial themes of Catholic faith is the struggle to contend with that sense of divine presence, which is perceived as real yet obscure, and, which is normally experienced as paradoxical. The heart of most interesting stories of conversion to Catholicism is the effort to grapple with the obscurity and paradox of a God present in the midst of a people who are less than godlike.

The word of God, then, is the word of One present within the church's life, as we have already noted. The word of scripture is a word about the life of God that breathes within the church. And the ministry of the word is not simply the ministry of preaching. According to the Introduction, ". . . in teaching, life, and worship the Church keeps alive and passes on to every generation all that it is, all that it believes" (No. 8). Moreover, this is not the static handing on of some abstract truth that is assimilated like a blueprint. The divine truth is God's life among God's people, and that is seen as something into which the church must live. The divine truth is not something held as a possession; it is a life that the church has the vocation to discover: ". . . with the passage of the centuries, the Church is ever to advance toward the fullness of divine truth until God's word is wholly accomplished in it" (No. 8).

This is why the Introduction especially underscores the work of the Holy Spirit, devoting a whole section to it. That work of the Spirit inspires us to a "hearing" of the word in the full sense, not just in the moment of liturgical celebration but in the whole of life. Carefully embracing both the individual and the communal, liturgy and life, the Introduction expresses a vision in which the proclamation of the word issues in a life that teems with the richness of diversity:

> "The working of the Holy Spirit precedes, accompanies, and brings to completion the whole celebration of the liturgy. But the Spirit also brings home to each person individually everything that in the proclamation of the word of God is spoken for the good of the whole assembly of the faithful. In strengthening the unity of all, the Holy Spirit at the same time fosters a diversity of gifts and furthers their multiform operation" (No. 9).

It is significant, too, that the character of the whole church as sacramental is underscored in the Introduction's conception of the ministry of the word. As might be expected in a Roman Catholic document, the special role of the ordained ministry is singled out. But this should not obscure the fact that the ministry of the word is not seen as simply the holding of the office of teaching by virtue of ordination. By speaking of the church's keeping alive its faith by "teaching, life, and worship" (No. 8), the Introduction is carefully underscoring the role of the unordained in the ministry of the word. The ministry of the word is the task of the whole church, not simply of the clergy. Even the office of teaching is not seen as limited to the ordained clergy, for the document clearly refers as well to those who have not been ordained, but who have been "entrusted with exercising the ministry"(No. 8). This is of special importance because it reflects an official willingness to learn from recent experience in the church: that as ordination is not necessarily a qualification for proclaiming the word, so also are many qualified who are not ordained.

The first chapter closes with a brief reflection on the relationship between the word of God and the mystery of the eucharist (No. 10). Much of what it says may appear self-evident to a generation accustomed to a full liturgy of the word with vernacular readings and homily before the celebration of the liturgy of the eucharist. Note should be made, however, of the appeal to the twenty-fourth chapter of the Gospel according to St. Luke (the story of the disciples on the road to Emmaus). The choice of this scriptural example is important, for the biblical story is an account of the disciples reflecting with the risen Lord on their own experience in the light of the biblical message. Once again, we are reminded that the proclamation of the word is not about an event from time past, but a bringing of the scriptural word to bear on the life of the assembly; it is the point of meeting between the assembly's experience and the written record of the experience of God's people.

It must be stressed that this assumes that the assembly has a life to reflect upon, and represents a call to see to it that the church so lives and acts as to make that life possible. It is generally assumed now that the liturgy of the word should touch "daily life." This is true enough, but the Introduction is asking for more than that. The Christian transformation of "daily life" is not something we are called to enter into simply as individuals, but as a new community of disciples. In the story of the disciples on the road to Emmaus, Christ is found present among them "in the breaking of the bread." But, as the story makes so clear, this of course assumes that they have reason for breaking bread together, that they have a common story to share that rises out of a common life together.

2
Word and Music are Central

At first sight, there is little that appears to be new in Chapter II (Celebration of the Liturgy of the Word at Mass) that has not already been said in previous official instructions, especially in the General Instruction of the Roman Missal. Still new however, and often undiscovered (and hence unexplored), are some of the most basic principles and assumptions underlying the directives of Chapter II. For example, the assertion that "Readings from Scripture and the chants between the readings form the main part of the liturgy of the word" (No. 11), seems plain enough. Yet despite the clear description in the Introduction (and other official documents) of the responsorial psalm and the gospel acclamation as *chants*, the use of music at these points remains in practice as an ornamental option, suitable perhaps for "solemn" or "special" occasions. By describing these segments as *chants*, the official books are stating a decided preference: they are articulating a *norm* for the manner of celebration of these segments of the mass rite.

Why, then, is so little compunction felt at letting the congregation recite these portions? Why, indeed are other (and less important) moments where congregational song is less necessary given musical accompaniment (e.g., the entrance of the priest and other ministers or the preparation of the altar and gifts) while these critical moments remain bereft of song? Why, indeed, can a paragraph like this one so easily sound like so much fuss about a minute point?

The reason we are able to ignore this perfectly clear norm so easily is that we tend to underestimate what is required for real communal participation in public prayer. The reasons for that failure are understandable, and worth exploring if we are to avoid continuing to make the mistakes we are making. The effort to restore "conscious, active, and full participation of mind and body" (the General Instruction of the Roman Missal's term for communal participation on the part of the people, cf. No. 3) did not begin with Vatican II. It began with the effort to restore the prayers and readings of the mass to the people through hand missals—vernacular translations of the Latin liturgy bound into prayer books that could be used as librettos to help people "follow" what the priest was saying at the altar. On the heels of this development came the "dialogue Mass"—with the people taking up the responses that had previously been reserved to the altar servers. Apart from the occasional (and very rare) use of vernacular hymns at mass (often they were expressly forbidden), music remained restricted to chants and Latin hymns sung by choirs. And this musical usage was reserved for special occasions —the single high mass on a Sunday and other solemn moments. The normal experience of mass was low mass, entirely without music. This meant, for all practical purposes, that "active participation" tended to be understood as "reciting responses." At the time of Vatican II, there had been precious little other Catholic experience of active participation in the liturgy in this country. Not only did "active participation" tend to mean "reciting responses," but we also had virtually no repertoire of popular chants designed specifically for the rite of mass. Even in official texts this alienation of music from popular participation was perpetuated: official translation after official translation appeared with no musical accompaniment. It is a sign less of liberality than of poverty of repertoire that there are no *required* chants for vernacular texts for the very parts of the liturgy that are described as chants in the official documents. The underdeveloped state of the ministry of cantors and choirs nearly a generation after Vatican II is a commentary on our general lack of appreciation of the role of music in a truly popular and communal liturgy.

This is a situation that calls for serious attention on the one hand, and patience on the other. It deserves serious attention because music is integral to "conscious, active, and full participation of mind and body," and the chants of the liturgy of the word are its most important "people's part." But if we are to take up the task of developing the chants of the liturgy of the word, then patience is needed to deal with the experimental situation in which we find ourselves.

Why can it be asserted that music is integral to "conscious, active, and full participation of mind and body?" As already suggested, the model of "making responses" constitutes something less than full participation. The model assumes that the liturgy is something that the priest carries out and to which the people give their assent by making "responses." This accurately describes the kind of liturgy we had when people were using hand missals or when they attended dialogue masses. But the liturgical reform of Vatican II went considerably further than restoring to the people a role in responding to the words and action of the priest.

The Constitution on the Sacred Liturgy defined the liturgy as the action of the whole church, clergy and laity (No. 5), and this principle is restated in the General Instruction of the Roman Missal: "The celebration of Mass is the action of Christ and the people of God . . ." (No. 1). This is why the official documents describe the priest as "president" rather than "celebrant": all, without exception are co-celebrants of the liturgy. The role of the laity, then, is far more than simply a matter of "responding": it is a matter of engaging fully in an action which is not done *for* them, but *by* them.

Because the liturgy of the word is structured as a set of readings with "responses"—"Thanks be to God," responsorial psalmody, gospel acclamations, pause of silence after the second reading— there is a strong temptation to understand the liturgy of the word simply as a dialogue between God and ourselves, with God as speaker and ourselves as respondents. But in Catholic tradition, the word of God is not so readily and absolutely identified with the word of scripture. The scriptures are themselves a response to the "hearing" of God's "word": they are the word of God in the words of human beings. The people of God are at one and the same time hearers and proclaimers of the word.

In the context of the liturgy of the word, the responsorial psalm and gospel acclamations are not simply "responses to the readings." They are, rather, modes of liturgical expression whereby the laity express their role in the celebration of the word. The normal correspondence between the responsorial psalm and the first reading and gospel on Sundays should be noted. The responsorial psalm constitutes a summation of the word for that day—containing echoes and resonances of these readings, and, in a real sense, summing them up. Indeed, if there is anything that may be named a "theme" in a mass, it is to be found in the antiphon of the responsorial psalm. That antiphon normally resonates vigorously with the heart of the first and third reading. Likewise, by joining in the gospel acclamations, the assembly assumes its role of announcing the good news of Christ. To acclaim is not simply to assent: it is to identify oneself as a co-participant, to take responsibility for what is happening. Doubtless, it is because of its perception of the assembly as co-proclaimers of the word that the Introduction insists so vigorously on the importance of the ministry of lay readers. Most significant, it indicates that even when there is an abundance of ordained ministers present, lay readers are still to read the lessons. The Introduction is deeply sensitive to the role that such readers play in representing the role of the laity in the proclamation of the word.

Briefly, then, the central portion of the liturgy of the word—the readings, the responsorial psalm, and gospel acclamations—constitute an event of co-celebrating the word in which all are called upon to enact their proper roles as sharing co-responsibility for the proclamation of the word. It is interesting that the liturgical norms cast the presider *solely* in the role of silent presider (except for the homily itself). The normative minister for the proclamation of the gospel is the deacon; and if more than one priest but no deacon is present, the priest other than the presider is to proclaim the gospel. This norm is intended to preserve the character of the liturgy of the word as an event of co-celebration, highlighting as it does the diversity of ministries in the church.

The need for appropriate musical elaboration of the central people's parts in the liturgy of the word should be apparent from what has just been said. The importance of a portion of the liturgy and of the role of the minister who carries it out is signaled by what is *done*, and by the things we use to do it. We solemnize the eucharistic prayer, as we honor the role of the priest—by a variety of reverential gestures, by the special vesture of the priest, and by the special place, construction, and decoration of the altar. It is fairly easy to know that the eucharistic prayer is important: it is normally carried out as if it *were* important, in a place that befits its dignity. To put it simply, then, if the singing of the responsorial psalm and the gospel acclamations are the people's role in the proclamation of the word, then they too need to look and sound important. If this is one of the key ways that they express their baptismal consecration in the liturgy, then that moment ought to appear as a sacred action of a holy people.

It scarcely needs a dissertation on ritual anthropology to note that communal recitation is an exceedingly weak vehicle for expressing the sense of a sacred moment. Just about the only things that recite effectively in gatherings of more than a dozen are brief stereotyped formulae (like the pledge of allegiance in civil ceremonies or, in church, the Lord's prayer or the response to "pray, my brothers and sisters"). Acclamatory or antiphonal materials are, to be blunt, wretched and boring when recited by a group. Imagine a group of high school students reciting "Go, team, go," and you have some sense of the poverty of the kind of practice we still tolerate in church.

One of the reasons for the continued impoverishment of the people's role in the liturgy is an excessive reliance on the vernacular hymn for music at mass. While a rousing hymn may on occasion call forth a real sense of involvement, there are serious limitations on the use of hymnody for the Catholic eucharistic liturgy. In the first place, the eucharistic liturgy (and this includes its liturgy of the word) is a sacramental action, an event. The most effective mode of public vocal participation in an action is acclamation (a simple fact that is true of both secular and religious rituals). And from a practical standpoint, the hymn is a drearily impractical vehicle of worship when the congregation lacks the support of a strong and rightly placed choir. We wax romantic about the impressiveness of Protestant hymnody, forgetting that in the first place those hymns accompany a service very different in spirit and shape from the eucharistic liturgy, and forgetting in the second place that we do not have a choir at most of our liturgies. And even when we do have one, it is banished to a loft. Besides being impractical, hymnody inevitably functions largely as "filler," mainly for "covering" processions (entrance, preparation of the altar and gifts, communion, and recessional). *Especially* if done well, such use of hymnody tends to distort the significance of liturgical roles. For example, the heart of the entrance rites in the liturgical books is the acclaiming of Christ present in the midst of the assembly. This is why the ordinary "penitential rite" may be supplanted on occasion by other rites—the blessing and sprinkling with holy water, the welcoming of a child and its family at baptism, the welcoming of a couple to be married, the greeting of the deceased at the funeral mass. These events may supplant the ordinary "penitential rite" because these, too, are ways of celebrating Christ present in the midst of the people of God. Yet in practice, the brightest moment at the beginning of mass is the procession of the clergy and other ministers. Thus the conventional parish opening of the eucharistic liturgy defines the beginning of the ritual as a clerical act—clearly contrary to the intentions of the *Roman Missal*. Paradoxically, while the most fundamental principles of the Missal are distorted out of recognition, we woodenly

and slavishly follow some of its least fortunate minor directives—e.g., reciting the penitential rite exactly as it appears in the
liturgical books, rather than asking how we might best accentuate
the assertion of the liturgical books that the liturgy is celebrated
by the whole assembly of the church.

If the eucharistic liturgy is to be experienced as a fully co-
celebrated rite with the laity as fully enfranchised co-offerers, as
No. 54 of the General Instruction of the Roman Missal so carefully
defines them, then there are some six spaces that cry out for
musical development—the opening litany after the exchange of
greetings between priest and people (the place presently occupied
by penitential rites and *Gloria*), the responsorial psalm and gospel
acclamation, the general intercessions, the eucharistic prayer acclamations, and the litany before communion (presently the Lamb
of God). This would not only vastly improve the quality of participation; it would also vastly simplify the whole task of doing
good music at Mass, to say nothing of simplifying planning tasks.
We could function very well at a mass with a single cantor; all we
would need is basic acclamatory and antiphonal materials that
could be easily remembered and familiar everywhere. It would be
possible to produce a relatively small and inexpensive yet
dignified official people's participation book, and therefore properly sign the importance of the people's role in the liturgy.

Some serious attention needs to be given to the question of
books for the people. The Introduction is critical of the conventional use of leaflet missals, though, as is appropriate for a document of this sort, that criticism is masked by positive assertions.
The Introduction (No. 37) expressly prohibits the use of such
leaflet materials as substitutes for lectionary, gospel book, or
sacramentary. But it carefully defines these leaflets as "printed for
the faithful's preparation of the readings or for their personal
meditation." By implication, it discourages the laity's use of
printed texts of the readings during the actual proclamation of the
readings. But however welcome these official strictures on leaflet
missals may be, they still do not address the issue fully.

One of the most important ways in which the dignity of
liturgical speech is signaled is by the use of official books. The
prayer and sacrifice at the altar are honored by the sacramentary,
and the proclamation of the word is reverenced by beauty and
sound crafting of lectionary and gospel book. Why not, then,
something of similar dignity in the people's hands for the part they
play in the liturgy? All too often, the rightful critique of participation aids—that they distort the meaning of liturgical action (e.g.,
by distracting the hearer from the actual proclamation of the

readings in the midst of the assembly, by substituting the dead letter for the living voice in the midst of the church)—ignores our
literate culture. The most important moments of life are sealed
with the signing of written documents, as "putting it in writing" is
the ordinary way we signal that something is of special importance. Because of this, the consignment of "people's parts" to mere
leaflets, or indeed to any sort of commercial publication, may well
reflect a serious lack of appreciation both of our own culture and
of people's needs for full and authentic participation. Indeed, the
popularity of the inferior sort of leaflet missal may reflect a sound
instinct: that people in a literate culture find the important and
significant enshrined in the printed word. In the absence of a
beautiful, well-crafted, and official "people's book," such inferior
substitutes may be rushing in to fill a vacuum.

The question of a people's liturgical book (which would include
all the materials necessary for sung participation—litanies, acclamations, antiphons and anthems, as well as some material of
lesser import for participation at mass, i.e., hymnal material) is not
merely a matter of aesthetics, nor even simply a matter of prac-
ticality. It is true that a bound volume could be more beautiful
than leaflets, and the appearance of provincial or regional
people's books 'could be more economical than the present
deplorable situation of freelancing. An official book could also
have the practical advantage of signaling more clearly what is
more important and what is less important in "people's parts"—a
matter on which many leaflets are notoriously weak. But the point
being made here is not merely aesthetic, and not only practical,
but theological and sacramental as well. If the people really do
constitute a sacred assembly, if Christ really is present "in the
assembly," if popular participation is co-celebration, and not simple assent to what the priest is doing, then the liturgical role of the
people needs to be expressed by clear, unmistakable marks of
reverence for that role. In a literate culture such as ours, the use of
an official people's book would help considerably to mark that
role of the people, as Protestants have known for centuries.

The need for a people's book is all the more heightened if other
directives of the Introduction are taken seriously. The Introduction indicates a preference for a diversity of books—one for the
lessons, one specially decorated for the gospels. Likewise, the proclamation of the readings is attended with ceremony—the lectern
is to be reserved for the biblical readings; the gospel book is to be
carried in procession from the altar, etc. Without the proper
ceremonial enhancement of the people's part in the proclamation
of the word (i.e., with suitable music and suitable books), the

liturgy readily becomes unbalanced, a clerical or ministerial event to which the people are only an appendage. We noted earlier that piety remains inattentive to the presence of Christ in the assembly. No wonder. We accord that presence so few marks of honor.

To say that we need an official people's book and to say that we need to give priority to the key people's parts (beginning litany, responsorial psalm, gospel acclamation, general intercessions, eucharistic prayer acclamations, pre-communion litany) is not to suggest that we have some ready-made repertoire which could be instantly canonized and made official in a people's book. This is an arduous (if potentially rewarding) task to be taken up, and one that has scarcely begun. Conventional parochial practice has settled for fitting in bits and pieces of mainly ornamental music (though hideously ornamental, as when an ill-prepared cantor attempts to drag an ill-prepared congregation through unfamiliar hymns). We have also been enslaved to a wooden use of official texts when it comes to the people's parts. More often than not, we settle for mere recitation. This is not because of a lack of talent on the part of musical leadership, nor, really, because of the resistance of congregations. It is because we have failed to look closely enough at what is required for a liturgy to be experienced as a true event of co-celebration. Singing the "Lord, have mercy" and the *Gloria* and the responsorial psalm and the gospel acclamation will not bring us to a renewed celebration of the word—not, anyway, if we stick to the currently available repertoire.

What, then, do we need? In the first place, we need a close look at the disparity between the fundamental principles so clearly enunciated in the General Instruction of the Roman Missal and in the Introduction to the lectionary, and the actual, prescribed materials provided (supposedly) so that those principles can be carried out in practice. As we have already noted a number of times, the liturgy of the word hinges on the understanding that Christ is present in the midst of the assembly. This cannot animate the liturgy of the word unless people have come to reverence and celebrate that presence. Having already noted that this demands a deeper appreciation of what it means to be consecrated people through baptism and confirmation, we must also note that this presence of Christ in the assembly needs to be reverenced and celebrated at every mass. This is the function of entrance rites: to savor, celebrate and acclaim that sacred presence in the midst of the assembly. Practically speaking, that would mean far less concern with the musical acclamation of the entrance of the clergy and other ministers, and far more attention to developing the sort of litanies that could be led by a cantor, litanies that would allow the congregation to acclaim that it is good to be there because Christ in the Spirit is there. It might well lead us to ask whether the present texts of the "penitential rites" and the *Gloria* are at all adequate for this purpose. The texts we use, after all, were never introduced into the Roman liturgy until that sense of the assembly as a presence of Christ had begun to fade from Catholic consciousness.

Having made a variety of suggestions about changes that need to be made in the ways we interpret the introductory rites in the official liturgical books, it may be useful to the reader to suggest what that might "look" like in actual practice. This cannot be done, however, without serious reflection on present practice, especially as it affects the "penitential rite" at the beginning of mass, and as it affects the current convention of having made the entrance procession of the clergy to the accompaniment of a song *de rigeur.* The latter is only a suggestion of the official books, *not a requirement.*

As this commentary has labored to make clear, the whole point of liturgical reform has been to clarify *in practice and experience* (what else can participation of "mind and body" mean?) that the liturgy is an action of the whole assembly. Moreover, as we have again labored to make clear, a Catholic understanding of the word is grounded in an understanding of God as the God of the Gathering. Celebration of the word is grounded in faith in the real presence of Christ in the assembly. All other modes of Christ's presence are for the unfolding of that presence. Christ is present *for* us, as the "words of consecration" so clearly and consistently affirm. Thus the officially stated function of the introductory rites—to make the assembled congregation a unified community (General Instruction of the Roman Missal, No. 24)—requires the reverencing, cherishing, and celebrating of that sacred presence. The ritual experience should say to people, "We are here because Christ is alive among us." Insofar as ritual statements about ministry are made, the ritual experience should say, "And those ministries exist only to bring us more deeply into that life of Christ among us." While Catholic traditions other than the Roman know nothing of a public penitential beginning of the eucharistic liturgy, there is nothing at all wrong with the acknowledgement of human sinfulness as part of the ritual experience of beginning mass. The eucharist, after all, is for us sinners, not for the exlusively saved or the perfectly religious.

Both a biblical understanding of the eucharist and the Western tradition vigorously support an understanding of the eucharist as the dining of sinners at the Lord's table. Both the contemporary experience of a human church and Vatican II's acknowledgement of the inherent sinfulness of the church on its earthly journey demand an honest liturgy. We celebrate the mystery of Christ present among a sinful people: this is the glory and the horror of our existence as church. So it is not a question of abandoning the now-entrenched Western tradition (it only dates from about the ninth century) of beginning mass with expressions of penitence. But it is a matter of calling into question rites that define the laity as simply passive and sinful subjects of the clergy's ministrations. When the brightest moment of the introductory rites is the song heralding the entrance of the ministers, and when that moment is followed by what can only sound like an acknowledgement of our distance from the living Christ, the laity are indeed being ritually defined as the passive and sinful subjects of the clergy's ministrations.

In terms of what the liturgical books actually require, only the most modest of changes would be necessary: the abandonment of the dreadful introduction, "in order to prepare to celebrate the sacred mysteries, let us call to mind our sins" (which points to what divides us rather than to what unites us), and the abandonment of the unfortunate translation of the acclamations *Kyrie eleison* and *Christe eleison* as "Lord, have mercy." The Greek *eleison* does literally mean "have mercy," but that is about as helpful as saying that the Latin *Dominus* (Lord) literally translates as "despot." The lost tender resonances of the original Greek *eleison* are those of a loving, merciful, receptive, healing presence. In English, "Lord have mercy" can only sound like the plea of unforgiven sinners, and in any case it identifies the assembly simply as sinners. Sinners we are, but also a consecrated people, holy by our baptismal calling: *forgiven* sinners. If we have to be ironclad ritual purists who will not depart one jot and tittle from the text, then let us use the original Greek. We are doing no reverence to tradition by distorting the *Kyrie* litany into an excuse for an examination of conscience—a point the almost never-consulted sacramentary variants on the litany try so valiantly to make clear.

And so we proceed to the unfolding of a scenario, an "ordinary," i.e., most Sunday or festal celebrations where (as is normally the case) the congregation lacks the resources of a full choir.

Some five to ten minutes before the scheduled time of beginning the liturgy, ministers begin to take their places in the sanctuary. The organist or other instrumentalists begin playing (not "practicing"—if that is done, it occurs before any of the other ministers appear). The ministers reverence the altar when they enter, and take their seats. There is no special arrangement to their order of appearance—they simply do not arrive all at once. The deacon (or whoever will proclaim the gospel) reverently takes the book of the gospels from its (decorated) place of storage and reverently puts it on the altar. When the appointed time for the liturgy arrives, the music stops and the presider rises from his chair and greets the people. Once the formal liturgical greetings have been exchanged, the deacon or another minister invites the assembly to begin a litany of praise: "Let us all rejoice in the Lord who is present to heal and save." The cantor moves to her podium, and intones, "Lord, you heal the contrite," to which the people respond in song, "Glory to you, Lord Jesus Christ." The litany moves in leisurely exuberance through nine or a dozen such invitations to acclaim the saving Lord. When its sounds have died away, the presider gestures to the assembly, says "Let us pray," pauses, and reads the opening prayer of the day.

From week to week, certain variations will appear: the priest may have a few introductory comments, which vary, as will the deacon's introduction to the litany. So also, the cantor's invitations to acclamation will show a certain variation. But the people can count on the tune and the words of their responses being seasonally stable. They will look forward to the exuberance of the Easter acclamation, or the haunting plaintiveness of the Advent chant, as they will relish the stark sobriety of the Lenten melodies. They will thank God for the end of the days when they had to be dragged through "practice" almost every Sunday.

Similar questions must be asked of the responsorial psalmody. It is not the psalms that are the problem, but their dismal execution. The singing of a psalm with an antiphon is *sometimes* quite appropriate. Some psalms would be better done with three or more voices—e.g., cantor, schola, and people, or cantor, reader, and people. Some, indeed, would be more effectively set out as metric hymns. Here, to be sure, we would need both a creative resetting of the psalms (already underway under the auspices of ICEL) and a people's psalter so as to allow them to be fully involved. Creative adaptation of psalmody to local use is heartily encouraged by the Introduction: "To foster the congregation's singing, every means available in the various cultures is to be employed" (No. 21).

Conventionally used responsorial psalm antiphons (somewhat imitative of Gregorian chant) are much too weak for serious congregational use. They lack the robustness that should be characteristic of popular acclamation. If composers have been inattentive to the need for more robust antiphons, it may be because of the common understanding of the responsorial psalm as a "response to the readings." But the name "responsorial" simply refers to the traditional mode of singing the psalm, not its liturgical character. The responsorial psalm is actually a fourth reading—which is why the Introduction, while insisting that the lectern should be reserved for biblical readings, directs the psalmist to sing from the lectern. Given the status of the psalm as a fourth reading, it is the means by which the people co-celebrate the proclamation of the word. The people's antiphon is to be understood as an acclamation, not a mere "response."

It would seem, too, that a special psalm book for the cantor, though not mentioned by the Introduction, would be a desirable feature of a renewed celebration of the liturgy of the word. In our liturgy, we mark roles by the use of special books. The role of the psalm as the "people's reading" demands that the special ministry that facilitates that event be marked out as well. One of the distinctive features of the Introduction is its prizing of the diversity of ministries in the liturgy of the word. Even the peculiar recommendation that readers be vested is a well intentioned effort to say that all the diverse ministries are important. It would thus be fully in harmony with the spirit and general intentions of the Introduction to create a special book for the psalmist.

No commentary on the proclamation of the word would be complete without something said about the "lectern." "Lectern" is perhaps an unfortunate translation of the Latin *ambo*, since we identify the "lectern" as a bookstand. A whole generation of church architecture has provided us with marble and metal equivalents of the classroom lecturer's bookstand. The Latin *ambo* more accurately describes, not simply a bookstand, but rather, *the place from which the word is proclaimed*. From this perspective, a "lectern" might well include two or three steps above the common level of the sanctuary floor, a well-crafted cupboard for the storage of the sacred texts, and an adequate provision for the placement of several books to be used by several readers (as during the proclamation of the Passion in Holy Week). The Introduction makes a variety of comparisons between lectern and altar: the general suggestion is that the "lectern"—i.e, the place of reading—should have sufficient prominence, both functionally and artistically, so that it enjoys a certain parity with the altar. For a fully renewed liturgy, we need much fuller "lecterns" and somewhat sparser altars. The common visual situation, in which the lectern is a mere appendage to the altar, is, from the point of view of the principles enunciated in the official liturgical books, a totally inadequate expression of the relationship between word and sacrament.

The special importance of the Gospel reading is signed by song and a variety of ceremonies. Special note should be taken of the Introduction's mention of the deacon taking the gospel book from the altar (No. 17), as well as the Introduction's decided preference that the introduction to the gospel and its ending (This is the Gospel of the Lord) be sung and answered with song. The gospel proclamation is the "high point" of the liturgy of the word, and as such deserves full sacramental enactment. That is to say, it is the proclamation in the midst of the assembly of the church, and it is done as part of the eucharistic liturgy. This moment, then, should be an evocation of the multiform presence of Christ—in assembly, in ministers, in word. It points, by the use of the altar, to the presence of Christ in the eucharistic sacrifice. Solemn ceremony without vigorous (and therefore necessarily sung) acclamation by the people tends to clericalize the event. Every effort should be made, therefore, to assure that this event is fully participatory. Gospel acclamation music that overplays the role of a choir is also to be avoided. At acclamatory moments, the strongest role should be taken by the people. In passing, it may be appropriate to observe, too, that we are paying far too little architectural attention to the placement of choirs. It should go without saying that the support of a choir's ministry is always desirable and sometimes necessary, especially in large assemblies. If choirs are to take this role of supporting the congregation, they need to be placed where they can be experienced as doing just that.

Since a fully participatory liturgy requires a ministering choir, it is desirable that it be as visible as any other ministry. In the experience of this writer, Dahlgren Chapel on the Georgetown University Campus in Washington, D.C., and St. Paul's Chapel on the campus of the University of Wisconsin in Madison (both of them ordinary parish church size), provide useful models. In Dahlgren Chapel, the choir is placed behind the altar, with the congregation on the three other sides. At St. Paul's the altar space is in the center of the chapel, with choir on one side and other ministers on the other, and the congregation on the other two sides, facing one another across the altar. The result is that when the choir sings, it becomes a real leader of the celebration of the assembly. This means, of course, that the decorum of the choir must be that of a minister, and that the movements and attitude of the choir must be those of ministers. A choir director would need to spend time developing this model and this function.

Note should be taken of the cautious little reference to "other symbols of reverence that may be customary" in the gospel procession. One would think, for instance, that certain forms of dance during the singing of the alleluia would come under this umbrella. It is, in any case, an explicit acceptance of local adaptations.

The Liturgy of the Word as Event of Prayer

To say that the liturgy of the word is designed to savor, celebrate, and explore the meaning of Christ present in our midst, is to say that it is an event of prayer. The point of underscoring the need to develop the people's song and ceremony is that it is liturgical prayer, i.e., prayer carried out by the whole community of the faithful. As already suggested, for the liturgy of the word to be a full experience of liturgical prayer, careful attention needs to be paid to the introductory rites and to the development of the responsorial psalmody and the gospel acclamation. Certain other elements of the liturgy of the word, however, also deserve more attention than they often receive. The Introduction actually devotes a special section to *silence* (No. 28), and rightly so. The liturgy of the word is an event of prayerful hearing, and hearing requires intervals of silence. Keeping in mind that the average parochial assembly is not a choir of monks, the Introduction sensibly recommends short intervals of silence before the liturgy of the word (i.e., immediately after the opening prayer), after the readings, and after the homily. In an ordinary assembly, half-minute pauses at these points will likely prove to be more effective than a single lengthy pause after the homily.

The use of the creed or profession of faith presents certain problems that are acknowledged but not solved by the Introduction. As the Introduction says, the creed "has as its purpose in the celebration of Mass that the gathered faithful may respond and give assent to the word of God heard in the readings and through the homily" (No. 29). There is everything to be said for such a prayerful interlude. It is an opportunity for the assembly to recapitulate in prayer (and, it is hoped, in song) what has been savored, celebrated, and reflected upon through the whole course of the liturgy of the word. There could be no more appropriate way to begin the closing of the liturgy of the word, and no more appropriate way to move forward to the celebration of the eucharist. One can scarcely fault, either, the aspiration that "before they begin to celebrate in the eucharist the mystery of faith they may call to mind the rule of faith." Unfortunately, neither the "Apostles'" nor the "Nicene" creeds (both approved by Rome as formulae for the profession of faith) serve those purposes very well. The Nicene creed is too long for congregational song and becomes rote recitation when it is not. The Apostles' creed may be sung or recited easily, but it scarcely relates very easily to "the word of God heard in the readings and the homily." It lacks sufficient seasonal reference.

Serious attention needs to be given to alternative creedal texts "in a formulary approved by the church" that can be sung with ease, reverence, and vigor. There are a variety of New Testament creedal formulae that better lend themselves to popular liturgical prayer and to the liturgical seasons. Why not, for instance, some version of the hymn from Phillippians 4 (Christus factus est) for the latter part of Lent? Or some portion of the Apocalyptic songs to the Lamb for Easter or Advent? In fact, many of the New Testament canticles or some portion of them, if set to music, would function as ideal professions of faith. Or for that matter, what about the *Gloria* for the Christmas season? Its present place in the mass is the result of historical accident. There is nothing in the basic structure of the mass that demands its present placement or its use every Sunday.

One of the greatest disappointments of liturgical reform is that one of its major goals has not been achieved—the experience of the eucharist as the action of the whole church. Much discussion revolves around a sense of a lack of participation in the "center and high point" of the eucharistic liturgy—the eucharistic prayer. Officially, the General Instruction of the Roman Missal not only defines the prayer as the "center and high point" of the entire celebration. It also carefully notes that the "meaning of the prayer is that the whole assembly offers the sacrifice" (No. 54). Usually, the blame for its being experienced as less than this is placed on presidential style, on lack of interest on the part of congregations, and on the eucharistic prayers themselves. We may indeed have some idiosyncratic presiders, some indifferent worshipers, and some prayers that represent less than deathless prose. But even if we had more carefully trained presiders, more alert parishioners, and shorter and more eloquent eucharistic prayers, the problem would not be solved. If the eucharistic prayer is the "center and high point" of the entire celebration, then people have to be brought to the center and raised to the high point. In other words, unless they already experience the liturgy as *theirs* before the eucharistic prayer, they will not experience the priest (as the General Instruction of the Roman Missal describes him) as speaking on their behalf, as representative of the assembly.

The development of popular participation in the liturgy of the word, then, is crucial to popular participation in the liturgy of the eucharist. If, in the language of the General Instruction of the

Roman Missal, we think of the eucharistic prayer as "center and high point," then we have to ask critical questions about the *circumference* and *base* of authentic "full, conscious, and active participation of mind and body," which leads to that center and high point. As we have labored to indicate in this commentary, "full, conscious and active participation of mind and body" finds its grounding in the affirmation of Christ's presence in the Spirit in the midst of the assembly—an affirmation in song and ceremony as well as in the ordered diversity of ministries. If the eucharistic prayer is to be experienced authentically as the prayer of the whole assembly, then the assembly must have emerged as a praying and proclaiming assembly *before* it finds itself gathered at the table of the Lord. The eucharistic prayer is, on the General Instruction's own principles, best understood as a grand summation of what the whole action of the eucharistic liturgy is about. This is impossible if the liturgy of the word does not unfold as an event of corporate, communal, and fully participatory prayer—as, indeed, an event of co-celebration and not simply an event attended by mere "responses." Thus the critical people's elements that are the major vehicles of their active participation—the litany in the introductory rites, the responsorial psalm, the gospel acclamation, the prayerful silences, and the profession of faith—deserve and demand full attention as integral parts of the liturgy. That full attention is impossible without adequate music—and "adequate" means both robust and within the resources of ordinary congregations (meaning, in many cases, congregations that do not have a choir or the resources of a full-time paid musician).

All of the above considerations are especially important when it comes to the development of the general intercessions or prayer of the faithful. The Introduction carefully underlines the special character of the intercessions as forming a kind of bridge between the liturgy of the word and the liturgy of the eucharist: "In these petitions, the people, exercising their priestly function, make intercession for all [a direct quote from the General Instruction of the Roman Missal] with the result that, as the liturgy of the word has its full effects in them, they are better prepared to proceed to the liturgy of the eucharist" (No. 30). We should note, too, that the Introduction, like the General Instruction that it repeats, carefully highlights the character of the prayer as an act of the entire assembly: it is an exercise of the priesthood of all believers, with the presider at his chair, and the deacon, another minister, or *some of the faithful* proposing intentions for the people's prayer. Without rehearsing a litany of all the abuses to which this frequently misunderstood and often misinterpreted event is subject, it must be noted that most of the principles highlighted by the General Instruction of the Roman Missal (Nos. 45-47) are generally ignored. Most of the conventional planning now in vogue concentrates solely on what the Introduction describes as the "proposing of intentions," and while giving a limited scope to these intentions, this planning gives an even more limited scope to the place of the prayer of the people or to the importance of a diversity of ministries. Present practice cries out for a reexamination of what we are doing, not because Rome demands it (which it does) but because that reexamination is called for if the prayer of the faithful is to be a genuine event of popular participation (which is why Rome is so insistent on reiterating its principles here).

What, then, needs to be reexamined? First of all, we can note that the Introduction envisages a set of petitions of rather wide scope. Five *categories* of petition are named as categories to be included as a rule in every Sunday or feast day intercession: the universal church, the local community, the world, those oppressed by any burden, and special categories of people. This assumes a fairly lengthy interlude of prayer, with a significant number of named intentions (at least, one would assume, a dozen to fifteen). Second, the proposal of the intentions is to be "short and phrased with a measure of flexibility"—in other words, to the point, though not necessarily finely polished. Third, those who propose the intentions are *not* the priest, but the deacon, "another minister" or "some of the faithful." The deacon traditionally had this role because the deacon traditionally had charge of the church's ministries of care and healing, especially its ministry to the poor. In a realistic bow to the present shape of ministry (including the ministry of women), this naming of the intentions is officially opened to those who now exercise such ministries and can call the assembly to them in prayer.

If we were to take seriously the principle of the General Instruction of the Roman Missal (and reiterated by the Introduction) that this moment of prayer is a significant exercise of the priesthood of all believers, we would pay more attention to the *central* issue in this prayer—how to make the role of the praying faithful significant. The conventional rehearsing of a litany of intentions with rapid fire "responses" from the congregation just does not do it. There is neither time for the faithful to pray over the intentions they hear proposed, nor an adequate way of signing publicly that what they are doing is the most important part of the prayer. There is, however, a simple way this could be done, within the resources of any assembly with a cantor. A minister would announce an intention, e.g., "For our holy father, Pope John Paul II." There would then be a moment's pause while the assembly digested the intention and made it its own. Then a cantor would sing, "Lord, we ask you, hear our prayer," or some other such versicle, and the people would acclaim, "Lord, hear us," or "Lord have mercy," or some other appropriate expression. Such a prayer of the faithful would tax neither the time of planners nor the talents of ministers nor the capacities of congregations, and all could pray as they now cannot. And if we had the courage to bid congregations to assume the classic and traditional position of praying with upraised hands when they joined in the litany of intercession, they might begin to experience the eucharistic prayer as resonating their own.

The whole point of the general intercessions, of course, is for the assembly to experience itself as a community concerned about the needs of others and to lift these concerns up in intercession. There is no absolute need for the people's part to be sung here, as long as the result is that people can experience this as *their* prayer and not merely as an assent to a minister's preoccupations.

3
The Word Proclaimed

In many ways, much of what is said in Chapter III has been sub-
sumed in commentary on the two preceding chapters. We should
observe, however, that this section lags behind the other two in its
conception of the celebration and proclamation of the word, and
in its receptivity to new developments in the life of the church.
This is not to say that this section is retrograde or oppressive: quite
the contrary. It vigorously upholds the principle of co-celebration
of the word by the whole assembly. Thus No. 40 makes it clear
that the use of lectionary options is not simply at the presider's
discretion, but should be the result of real consultation. It assumes
a laity actively involved in planning as well as in celebration, and
it assumes that they are intelligent and informed. Likewise, No. 52
deals creatively with the fact that as long as women may not be instituted as readers, some communities will refuse to let them read.
It is quick to encourage the ministry of readers that have not been
instituted—a tacit acceptance of what has become widespread
local practice.

Still, we may regret the now-tired notion that the commentator
has a genuine liturgical ministry. Experience has shown that this
may be useful on occasion (e.g., when there is a significant number
of people present who are unfamiliar with the liturgy), but, on a
regular basis, the commentator is a didactic nuisance.

We might also regret that Chapter III in effect describes the
presider as an active agent in the proclamation of the word and
the people as passive agents. We might also have hoped to hear
more about those not ordained "who have been entrusted with

that ministry" of proclaiming the word in preaching (No. 8). This is an unrestricted opening to the ministry of women/lay people as preachers in the assembly, and comes as a stunning echo of the more cautious and restricted statement in the *Directory for Masses with Children* (No. 24) that those who have the gift (but not necessarily ordination) may preach at masses with children.

Considering, however, the Introduction's general openness to local practices that did not develop under Rome's initiative, the theoretical dichotomy between priest as active agent of proclamation and people as passive hearers should not be taken as a brake to local initiative, but as reflective of the "state of the art." In most large assemblies, we have not found a way to make preaching a more dialogical event. It is interesting to note that, for all its hazards (even more likely to be noted by Rome than by its advocates) the "dialogue homily" is nowhere singled out for criticism, though a variety of other practices (e.g., the use of leaflet missals) are gently criticized. When these considerations are joined to the strong exhortation to the laity to become involved hearers of the word, we are led to the inevitable conclusion that Chapter III is tentative rather than restrictive. It has to be tentative because a viable "dialogue homily" for a large assembly has not yet been developed—at least not as an imitable model.

The already harried preacher may well ask "Who needs it?" But the point is we do need it. The most frequent criticism of homilies is that they do not touch "ordinary life." Anyone who knows priests knows how absurd it is to assume that the fault lies with their being out of touch with "ordinary life." It is also doubtful that the real failure is a failure of preaching technique. If homilies are out of touch with "ordinary life" it is because the very structure of the homily is alien to our culture. A speaking situation where there is no spoken response from the hearers is simply unknown to us—unknown, anyway, as a viable and satisfactory means of communication. Even televised presidential speeches are followed by a round of commentary. In a culture where it is assumed that the majority of adults are at least functionally literate and responsible agents in society, a situation structured for monologue quietly overheard is perceived as at best authoritarian and dictatorial; at worst, pedantic and boring. The monological homily may have worked in classic antiquity—but even there, we know that congregations at least booed, cheered, laughed, and wept, just as they did during the supposedly benighted middle ages. Given the cultural context of general literacy and responsibility, and a liturgy where (at least in principle) co-celebration on the part of the laity is vigorously encouraged, the homily needs to be recast in a more dialogical mode. Yet the conventional meanderings simply will not suit a large assembly. The size of the group demands a structure of co-proclamation.

Here, clearly, a lay ministry of preaching needs to be developed. In every other area of the eucharistic liturgy, co-celebration is the rule rather than the exception. We should note, especially, the general preference for including the deacon's ministry in liturgical celebration, as well as the Introduction opening that ministry in the direction of lay people by constantly speaking of "or another minister" (including, by implication, especially because they are not expressly excluded, women). The homily might well come to life (and touch "ordinary life") if it were co-celebrated—shared by the priest and one or two other ministers. Standing alone, the homily is too easily perceived as an expression of wooden orthodoxy. If it were accompanied by two or three well-reflected responses from representatives of the assembly, it could well appear again as a life-giving word of proclamation.

4
The Liturgical Year

Most of what is contained in Chapters IV and V speaks for itself: it simply describes the contents of the lectionary. But there is a certain danger of losing the forest by looking at all the trees. Two things require comment: the basic reason for the arrangement of scripture special to the lectionary, and the fundamental spirit of the reformed liturgical year. Neither of these seem to be adequately understood, partly because they are not adequately articulated by the official documents themselves. This is not to say that the Introduction neglects a basic principle for the arrangement of the lectionary or that it ignores the spirit of the new liturgical year. It is only to say that it fails to articulate its own most basic presuppositions. What follows is an effort to do just that: to make explicit what is implied by the Introduction.

The liturgical year is shaped to celebrate, as the Introduction so often asserts, "the mystery of Christ," that is, to call us to an ever-deeper understanding of Christ crucified, risen, and present in our midst in the power of the Spirit. The reform of the year—the most important item on that agenda being the reform and enrichment of the lectionary—reflects a move away from what is technically known as the "historicization" of the church year. Many of the practices of piety in the past, including a variety of practices eventually enshrined in the official liturgy, were subject to that historicization. That is to say, the liturgical year, especially its major festal seasons, tended to be seen as a "following the footsteps of Jesus," beginning with the hope of his birth, through his infancy, into his public ministry, (in Lent and Holy Week) through each moment of his passion, then in the Easter season through his resurrection ministry, and on to the coming of the Spirit at Pentecost. The major moments of the liturgical year looked like a schema to trace those footsteps in detail. A naive reading of the Sunday gospels in sequence through the great festal seasons tends to reinforce that view of the liturgical year.

In the years before Vatican II, however, scripture study and liturgical history began to point up the inadequacy of this understanding of both the New Testament and of the liturgical year. There was a rediscovery of the resurrection as the center both of New Testament Christianity and of the liturgy. The resurrection was the event that constituted the early church: it was not simply something that "happened to Jesus." Rather, Jesus, in rising from the dead, raised with him a new community in the Spirit. The resurrection happened to Jesus *and the disciples.* And in their gatherings together to search the scriptures, to pray, and to break the bread of the eucharist, that new community discovered the risen Lord present in its midst.

The books we have come to call gospels were generated out of that experience of the risen Lord. The telling and retelling of stories of the life of Jesus was not to produce a detailed novel about One who was now absent, but to probe what it meant that the One crucified and risen now lives in the Spirit among God's people. Gospel stories are not simply stories about Jesus: they are stories of the church in its encounter with the risen Lord. Sunday became known as "the Lord's day," less as a commemoration of the past event of the resurrection than because this was the day the church chose to assemble to rekindle the experience of the risen Lord. The liturgical year found its starting point in that weekly communal celebration of the resurrection.

Liturgical reform aimed at a restoration of that wholeness: the bringing together of the assembly of the faithful to renew itself for its mission in the world by savoring and celebrating the presence of the Lord in its midst. Every Sunday is a renewal of the primordial experience of a community that knows Christ crucified and risen, present in the Spirit to heal, save, and empower. But lectionary reform can only be understood in the context of the reform of the eucharistic liturgy itself. In that reform, there is a call to the assembly to redefine itself, a call that has been put forth under the rubric of "full, conscious, and active participation" (cf. General Instruction of the Roman Missal, Chapter I). What does that redefinition mean? It does not mean simply that the people are called to better "follow along" the action of the priest through the use of the vernacular language, simpler gestures, the priest facing the people, the people singing songs, etc. Rather, the point of that redefinition is that the eucharist is the action of the *entire assembly* (cf. General Instruction of the Roman Missal, Chapter 1). The priest is present because the assembly is present, not the other way round. The catechetics and ritual of the past tended to give the impression that the major business of the eucharist is to make present an absent Jesus. The point of reform of the eucharistic rite is to make clear that, on the contrary, we come together to make manifest Christ already present. The eucharistic action is the proclamation of the gospel *par excellence*; by that action we affirm what it means that Christ is risen from the dead and alive in the Spirit. And the function of the lectionary is to unfold that meaning Sunday by Sunday. It unfolds what it means to "Do this in memory of me."

A. The Sunday Eucharist as Proclamation of the Gospel

The starting point for understanding the reformed cycle of the church year, then, is an understanding of the major lines of eucharistic reform. We are not there to "remember the Lord" as he was once upon a time, far away, and long ago, but as he is in and for the life of the community of faith, working among us by the Spirit. The heart of Jesus' own ministry was that he welcomed the sinner and the outcast, and ate at the table with them. The heart of the resurrection experience of the disciples was that they discovered themselves brought together as a forgiven and reconciling community. The eucharistic celebration is so shaped as to allow the assembly to identify itself as sharing in that reconciling community of the disciples gathered at the Lord's table.

This is self-evident in the gestures of sharing (the people singing and speaking aloud, the ministers facing the people, the exchange of the peace, communion in the hand, communion from the cup) that have been characteristic marks of liturgical reform. But the meaning of these gestures is often not appreciated in sufficient depth because we bring the relics of a pre-Vatican II piety to them. We are literally not able to hear the prayers we use (the very prayers which interpret these gestures) because we use new prayers with unrenewed ears. The General Instruction, for instance, describes the eucharistic prayer as the "center and high point" of the entire eucharistic celebration (Cf. No. 54), but this is generally not the experience of the assembly. Some of this has to do with poverty of celebration (e.g., the almost total abandonment of song for the preface and its preceding dialogue, the use of inadequate music for the acclamations, or none at all). But what a

liturgical act means to people has everything to do with the
perceptions people bring to it. Poverty of celebration may be as
much a symptom as a cause of a lack of full understanding of the
eucharistic prayer.

And so we need to identify those relics of pre-Vatican II piety
that cripple a fuller and deeper understanding of the present
eucharistic liturgy. We likewise need to identify the distinctive
characteristics of our present prayer pattern that speak for the
recovery of a richer and more traditional (i.e., faithful to the whole
tradition, including biblical tradition) understanding of what it
means to gather for eucharistic celebration. What, then, are those
relics of pre-Vatican II piety?

The first of those relics is that the assembly is identified as a
community "following" the action of the priest. This tends to
define the individual worshiper as a solitary spectator in a crowd
of spectators (something fostered by our architecture, as well as by
the way we often use our present liturgy). Our present prayers and
gestures, however, define the assembly as active agent in the
liturgy, and the individual worshiper is seen, not as a solitary spectator, but as a co-offerer and co-celebrant of the eucharist. This is
why the official books speak of the priest as "presiding" or
"presider," not as "celebrant." We are all celebrants. As the
General Instruction asserts, the meaning of the eucharistic prayer
is that "the whole congregation offers the sacrifice" (No. 54). This
has important consequences for our perceptions of what we do
and say at the eucharist. "Do this in memory of me" becomes (as it
was originally intended, and as it is now being said with the priest
facing the assembly) an invitation addressed to all.

The "this" of "Do this in memory of me" is not the priest's
saying of the words of consecration over the bread and wine (important as that may be), but the action to which Jesus referred: the
taking of bread and wine (preparation of the altar and gifts), the
giving of thanks and praise (eucharistic prayer), and eating and
drinking together (holy communion). We present bread and wine
in thanksgiving; we share the bread of life and the cup of salvation. These are the fundamental gestures of the eucharistic action
over which the eucharistic prayer is said as interpretation of what
we are doing.

If gestures like the exchange of the peace are experienced as "in-
trusions" or "distractions" or as the "priest's greeting," it is
because we have failed to grasp fully that the sacred action takes
place not simply at the hands of the Priest, but in the midst of the
whole assembly. Parenthetically, it may be noted that we need a
renewed architecture that will make it visually and kinesthetically

unmistakable that the whole assembly is gathered around the altar.[1]

The second relic of pre-Vatican II piety, integrally related to the perception of the individual worshiper as solitary spectator, is the notion that the priest "represents Christ." This is not to suggest that the priest does not "represent Christ," but to note that by itself it is an inadequate and limiting interpretation of what the eucharist is about. The General Instruction of the Roman Missal (as well as a number of other equally important official documents) speaks of Christ present "in the assembly" as the *first* representation of Christ, and goes on to speak of Christ, present not simply in his representation by the priest, but as represented by *all* the ministers (Cf. General Instruction, Chapter 1). According to the General Instruction, the lector, the acolyte, and the people in the back pew all "represent Christ." The whole point of our coming together in prayer and action is that we "represent Christ" to one another. An exclusive concentration on the priest as "representing Christ" tends to define the assembly as somehow separated from Christ. Yet the whole point of gathering for eucharist is that we are identified with Christ. Christ is present on the altar because Christ is present in the pew. This is why all orations are offered "through Christ our Lord," and why the eucharistic prayer is offered "through him, and in him, and with him": the point of eucharistic gathering is to identify ourselves with Christ. The function of the priest's prayers and gestures is (a) to *invite* the assembly to that identification (this is why we are constantly greeted, "The Lord be with you"); and (b) to *interpret* the meaning of that identification (the major prayers of the priest—opening prayer, prayer concluding the general intercessions, eucharistic prayer, prayer after communion—are interpretations of what the *whole assembly* is doing).

Even as a community of sinners, we "represent Christ," i.e., are a sacramental presence of Christ to one another. By naming ourselves as a community of sinners in pleas for God's mercy (penitential rites, Lamb of God, "Lord I am not worthy," etc.), we are naming the assembly of the faithful as a place where it is safe to acknowledge our sinfulness, and by so doing, we are naming it

---

[1]This *can* be achieved for a large assembly, and it can be achieved in the remodeling of an old space. Dahlgren Chapel on the Georgetown University campus and St. Paul's Chapel on the University of Wisconsin campus in Madison are excellent examples. Among new buildings, Our Lady of Nazareth in Roanoke, Virginia is a fine example of true post-Vatican II architecture in terms of the visual and kinesthetic relationship of altar to assembly.

as a place where God's mercy in Christ is accessible. In uttering penitential pleas, we are at the same time making promises to one another to be a community of welcome and reconciliation for the sinner. The dreary wallowing in guilt that often distorts these utterances ("For the times we have . . . . Lord, have mercy") reflects a failure to grapple with what it means to pray for the mercy of God in the presence of one another. Likewise, musical interpretations of the "penitential" litanies (Lord, have mercy, Lamb of God)—which make of them simple pleas for pardon and which do not make of them a resonance of the voice of the forgiving Lord—represent serious distortions of the character of prayer in common as an identification with the Lord and a promise to live by that identification. The point of liturgical speech is that it is speech in the hearing of one another. Just as in the proclamation of biblical texts we are called to hear the word of God in the words of God's people, so also in the proclaiming of prayer aloud, we are called to hear God's promise in the pleas of God's people.

The nature of the action of the eucharist as representing Christ to one another, and the nature of liturgical prayer as speaking for our identification with Christ and for our promise to be Christ for one another, can best be explored by reflection on the reform of the eucharistic prayer, best represented in Eucharistic Prayers III and IV of the sacramentary.[2] The most obvious features of that reform are the use of the prayer in the language of the people and uttered in their hearing, the restoration of the first half of the prayer as a thanksgiving narrative, the inclusion of invocations for the work of the Spirit (epiclesis), and the insistence that the people are to join in by acclamation.

It will be useful to begin with acclamation, for the simple reason that it is the least understood of our "new" (i.e., restored to use since Vatican II) prayer forms. The definition of the assembly as an audience of spectators has been kept alive by the use of the analogy of applause for understanding the nature of acclamation. Applause *can* be a form of acclamation, but not all forms of applause are acclamations, and in any case it is culturally impermissible for most Roman Catholics to applaud as a form of acclamation in prayer. It smacks too much of the theater and the sports arena. Acclamation is a political act, the act of enfranchised participants. In medieval England, for instance, the popular ac-

---

[2]For reasons which should be self-evident from the commentary that follows on the reform of the eucharistic prayer, Sunday use of eucharistic Prayer I is pastorally irresponsible. Prayer II is not (according to the sacramentary) to be used on Sundays and Holy Days.

claiming of a new king was more critical to the legitimacy of his succession to the throne than his coronation. It represented the people taking ownership of him as their king. In a variety of contemporary contexts, vote by acclamation is as acceptable as vote by ballot or show of hands: indeed, it often overrides ordinary rules of procedure. Liturgical acclamations, then, are not simply "responses": they are the verbal acts by which we take ownership of prayerful utterances. By acclaiming, we take responsibility for the prayer: we make it our own and affirm that it speaks for us.

In the Roman rite, the major eucharistic acclamations are the sanctus (Holy, holy, holy Lord) and great amen. The point of the solemnity of the preface and doxology (the measured cadences of their language[3] and—at least in terms of norm—their being sung, as well as the solemn elevation of the consecrated gifts at the doxology[4]) is that preface and doxology are designed to lead the assembly into a moment of affirmation: the priest prays the preface *so that* the whole assembly can enter into the sanctus wholeheartedly; he prays the doxology *so that* the people can give a wholehearted and fullthroated amen. Much of our sanctus and great amen music currently in use[5] fails to respect the solemnity of these moments. The sanctus is based on Isaiah 6: the story of the call of the prophet to God's service. The preface is thus a call to the assembly to take ownership of its own calling as a people gifted and chosen. We are invited to sing "with angels and archangels and the whole company of the heavenly host" as the agents of God's work on earth, a task that is at the same time joyous, serious, and awesome. And in so identifying ourselves as God's

---

[3]This is somewhat obscured in many preface translations, and perhaps somewhat obscured by the recent attempt to cram too much into the thanksgiving of the preface. The preface is less a full thanksgiving than an invitation to it. The terse thanksgivings of the festal prefaces of the old Roman Missal and the general praise of the invariable preface of Eucharistic Prayer IV are far better forms than the verbose and over-specific new prefaces which have been introduced. Presiders who embroider the preface with further thanksgivings, or who substitute variable prefaces for the preface of Prayer IV betray a misunderstanding both of the nature of the preface and of their own ministry at the altar. Their task is not to "lead" thanksgiving, but to lead people into it.

[4]It should be noted that according to the directions of the sacramentary, the "major" elevation of the gifts takes place at the doxology: it is supposed to be visually more dramatic than the elevations at the consecration. The priest is *not* instructed to elevate the gifts to anything beyond breast height at the consecration.

[5]To say nothing of the continued usage of recitation, abetted mainly by our not having a singable repertoire of solid acclamatory music for congregations that have something less than the services of a full choir or an extraordinarily able cantor.

servants on earth, we are identifying with the Christ who is servant of all. How much contemporary preface proclamation and
sanctus singing conveys the weight of that affirmation for a congregation? Similarly, the great amen follows the doxology, which
affirms that it is through Christ, with Christ, and in Christ that we
are gathered as a people. We are saying amen not simply to
Christ's presence under the forms of bread and wine, but amen to
the purpose for which Christ is present under those forms: for us to
be the manifestation of Christ's presence in the world. In a word,
we are saying amen to our calling as Christians.

The function of the acclamations—as affirmation of our calling
as Christians, and as communal vow formulas uttering our promise to live according to that calling—is better understood if we
recognize the purpose of the restoration of the thanksgiving series
to the eucharistic prayer. That series is succinct in Prayer III, more
expanded in Prayer IV:

Prayer III

Father, you are holy indeed
and all creation rightly gives you praise.
All life, all holiness comes from you
through your Son, Jesus Christ our Lord,
by the working of the Holy Spirit.
From age to age you gather a people to yourself,
so that from east to west
a perfect offering may be made
to the glory of your name.

Prayer IV

Father, we acknowledge your greatness:
all your actions show your wisdom and love.
You formed man in your own likeness
and set him over the whole world
to serve you, his creator,
and to rule over all creatures.
Even when he disobeyed you and lost your friendship
you did not abandon him to the power of death,
but helped all men to seek and find you.
Again and again you offered a covenant to man,
and through the prophets taught him to hope for
    salvation.
Father, you so loved the world
that in the fullness of time you sent your only Son to be
    our Savior.
To the poor he proclaimed the good news of salvation,
to prisoners, freedom

and to those in sorrow, joy.
In fulfillment of your will
he gave himself up to death;
but by rising from the dead,
he destroyed death and restored life.
And that we might live no longer for ourselves but for
   him,
he sent the Holy Spirit from you, Father,
as his first gift to those who believe,
to complete his work on earth
and bring us the fullness of grace.

The point of giving thanks for the great events of salvation history is not to give God thanks for events that happened in some remote or mythic time past, but to identify ourselves as that people among whom the Spirit of God moves and works. The biblical history is ours because it is the same God who is in our own midst. The invocation of the Spirit naturally flows from the thanksgiving, both as acknowledgement of the work of that Spirit among us, and as plea for the fulfillment of that work. The prayer for the consecration of the gifts is at the same time a prayer for the consecration of the assembly. Because God is at work among us, we can pray here and now for the manifestation of that work in our midst, and for its fulfillment. Christ is made present under the forms of bread and wine for the sake of our being the full presence of Christ in the world. This is why the offering language of the prayers expands into a "communion epiclesis," an invocation of the Spirit, praying that by sharing the body and blood of Christ we will become a "perfect offering":

Prayer III

Grant that we, who are nourished
by his body and blood, may be
filled with his Holy Spirit,
and become one body, one spirit
in Christ. May he make us an
everlasting gift to you . . .

Prayer IV

Lord, look upon
this sacrifice which you have
given to your Church; and
by your Holy Spirit, gather
all who share this bread
and wine into the one body
of Christ, a living
sacrifice of praise.

When the eucharistic prayer is understood from the perspective of acknowledgement, as utterance of the assembly's grateful sense of identification with Christ by the work of the Spirit, then we are better enabled to perceive the institution narrative (recital of the story of the Last supper) and the anamnesis (Summary recital of what we are doing: "offering sacrifice," i.e., identifying ourselves as God's own people "in memory" of Christ's death and resurrection, identifying ourselves as a people among whom and in whom, by the Spirit, Christ's death and resurrection are lived out) and the "anamnesis acclamation" that comes between them.[6] The point of the narrative is not simply to consecrate the bread and the wine, but to sum up the meaning of the whole prayer, that by doing "this" (i.e., presenting bread and wine, giving thanks and praise in acknowledgement of our calling, sharing together at the eucharistic table), we are identified as a community of disciples gathered around the table of the risen Lord. And the anamnesis, with its language of sacrifice, underscores the fact that our doing this "in memory" of Jesus is not a mere mental recalling of him, but is, rather, an actual participation in his saving activity.

From what we have said about the nature of the eucharistic action and about the nature of the eucharistic prayer as interpreting that action, it should be self-evident that there is an intimate and indeed integral connection between the proclamation of the word and the celebration of the eucharist. The eucharistic prayer sums up what is proclaimed in the celebration of the word. The task of liturgical preaching, as of planning, becomes one of making a threefold link between biblical story, prayer of the church, and the living experience of the assembly. We come together to celebrate our own grace, to be reconciled to our own brokenness, and to find these in the context of the biblical story.

Preachers and planners must be as attuned to the sin and grace of the assembly as they are to what our prayers and scriptures are saying about the assembly. Their task is to invite people to grasp the connections between the life of the assembly, the word proclaimed, and the prayers and gestures we use.[7] In the experience of

---

[6]Somewhat unfortunately. The placement of the anamnesis acclamation before the priest's words interpreting what we are doing "in memory" of Jesus Christ tends to tie it too much to the preceding narrative. The congregation gets the impression either that the function of the acclamation is to adore Christ present under the forms of bread and wine or to "think about" Christ's death and resurrection as historically past events. The acclamation would be better placed after the anamnesis.

[7]More detailed commentary on the meaning of the eucharistic prayer and other gestures can be found in *Mass In Time of Doubt* (NPM: 1983).

this commentator, much of our present music too sweetly and cheaply names us as graced, too much of our present preaching is more attuned to our sin than to our grace, and neither calls us very effectually or vividly to an awareness of ourselves as a community making promises to one another. This is more the result of ignorance than of negligence—ignorance of the structure of the eucharistic celebration as action of the assembly, ignorance of the nature of the prayers and biblical texts that interpret that structure, and ignorance of the shape of the lectionary. Both the ministry of music and the ministry of preaching interpret the meaning of assembling for eucharist. If the musical stress is on the ornamental rather than the acclamatory (strong hymns and weak acclamations), or if preaching ignores the connection between eucharist celebrated and life lived, then the event of celebration as action of the assembly breaks down. The awareness of ourselves as a community making promises to one another is obscured and diminished. And assuming that they are attuned both to the sin and grace of the communities that they serve, then the critical planning question, for musician as for preacher, is not simply "What is today's gospel," but "How do we identify Christ in the gospel with Christ in the assembly?"; "What is the relationship between gospel and eucharistic prayer?"; and "How do they relate to the lives of this assembly of God's people?"

B. The Rhythm of Feasts and Seasons

The function of the Sunday lectionary, then, is to unfold what it means to gather to celebrate the eucharist together—an unfolding of what is known as the "paschal mystery." This is accurately, but perhaps too easily summed up as celebrating "Christ's death and resurrection." Because of the historicization of the church year, which we noted earlier, there is a tendency to perceive "Christ's death and resurrection" simply as past events, and not to recognize that the point of celebrating them is that we are the community called to identification with Christ dead and risen. All feasts find their center in the Sunday celebration of the eucharist, and they find it there because that is where the assembly of the faithful comes together. The two great festal seasons (Advent-Christmas-Epiphany and Lent-Easter) are best understood as unfolding the meaning of the Sunday assembly for eucharist. Planning and preaching that treat the liturgical year as a linear series, or worse, as a discrete series of lectionary texts to be taken Sunday by Sunday without any relation to one another, miss the point of the Sunday center. Every Sunday is a summation of the whole Gospel. This lays bare the fallacy of preaching and planning by

"theme" alone. There are, of course, certain "themes" that can be
traced, especially on special feasts or during the great seasons
(Advent-Christmas-Epiphany or Lent-Easter-Pentecost). But exclusive attention to "theme" reduces the lectionary to a very ar-
bitrary lesson plan, and thins celebration to a very awkwardly
contrived event of information-imparting. It also breaks down
totally during "Ordinary Time" when there is a sequential reading
of gospel and epistle without thematic relation to one another.

From the perspective of the planner, the preacher, and the
minister of music, then, it is not enough to consult the lectionary
and sacramentary of the day. Some perspective is needed on the
function of the readings and prayers of the day in relation to the
great seasons. From the perspective of planning, preaching, and
music, understanding begins, not at the linear beginning, (e.g., the
First Sunday of Advent), but at the center; that is, the Sunday
celebration (Eucharistic prayer and people's action) moving outward to the great Sunday of the year, Easter, and to its
"echo"—Christmas-Epiphany. Think, if you will, not of a line with
special red dots on it, but of concentric circles, with Sunday at the
center, the paschal celebration around it as its natural outflow,
and Christmas on the next ring as a resonance of the paschal
celebration. The sequential "Ordinary Time" would form the
outer circle.

If there is a connection between Sunday eucharist and the great
festivals, there is also a connection between the great festivals and
the seasons that precede and follow them. Christmas unfolds by
anticipation back into Advent and finds its fullness in Epiphany
and (though much neglected) the Feast of the Purification of the
Lord (Candlemas). Likewise, Easter unfolds by anticipation back
into Lent and finds its fullness in the celebration of Pentecost. We
have not understood Advent if we have not understood Christmas,
and we do not understand Pentecost if we have not understood
Easter. The best way to obtain a synopsis of what a liturgical
season is about is to ponder the liturgical texts (especially those of
the lectionary) of the *vigil* that constitutes the finale of the season.
A vigil, while it looks forward to a coming season, is also a
retrospect, a grand summation of what has gone before. The fact
that few people attend the vigil masses of Christmas or Pentecost
should not deter us from searching the texts of these days to un-
cover the fundamental meaning of the Advent and Easter Seasons.
Just as the Easter vigil recapitulates the meaning of Lent, the other
great vigils recapitulate the seasons that they close. And while the
Christmas season has no vigil to close it, it does have the celebration of the Presentation of the Lord. Its celebration of the rising

hope for the nations in the midst of Israel constitutes the proper finale of the Christmas season.

None of these interconnections can be drawn seriously without recourse to biblical commentary, but it will be useful here to note some of the major lines of the interconnections. The historicization of the church year still governs most planning and preaching. We are still being called to "wait for the birth of Jesus" during Advent, to "follow Christ" during Lent, and to "pray for the coming of the Spirit" at the end of the Easter season. But these are woefully inadequate interpretations of what we are about when we come together for eucharistic celebration. Inadequate as these invitations are, they are not entirely inaccurate descriptions of the point of the great feasts and seasons. But left by themselves, they tend toward a separation of the believer from Christ rather than toward an identification. Advent is too easily reduced to a commemorative "let's pretend," a mere reflection back on the historic Israel's time before Christ. Christmas is sentimentalized into an admiring of the divine child. Lent degenerates into a punishing of ourselves for what happened to Christ. And the Easter season evaporates into a mythic time past. Where then is Christ present in the assembly? How then can it be said that the eucharistic prayer is the center and high point of the entire eucharistic celebration? And what then is the sacrifice offered by the "whole congregation"?

The point of the great feasts (as of the eucharist itself) is that the story of Christ has become our story. Dead, Jesus lives only in the memory of the community of disciples; risen, he is alive in our midst; coming again, he is our future. We experience Christ only by the working of the Spirit among God's people. It will be useful, then, to sketch here the ways in which the great feasts and seasons are intertwined with one another.

Since Easter is the great Sunday—amplifying the meaning of every Sunday, with its vigil summing up the meaning of Lent—it will be useful to begin there. The use of the Anglo-Saxon "Easter" as a translation of the Latin *pascha* (passover) somewhat obscures the nature of this night as a paschal vigil, the passover of Christians. It is also at heart a baptismal vigil, as the blessing of the font and the renewal of baptismal promises (even when there are no baptisms) should make abundantly clear. The celebration of the vigil as a Christian passover is self-evident from the texts: the reading from Exodus 14 about the crossing of the Red Sea may never be omitted, and the prayers over both candles and font make ample reference to that event.

Traditional commentary describes the crossing of the Red Sea as a "type" of Christian baptism. This has usually been understood as if what happened to Israel of old is a kind of "prefiguration" of what happens to Christians now. As Israel was saved and made into a nation by its passage through the Red Sea, we are made a new people through the waters of baptism. Besides this kind of thinking being uncongenial to contemporary worshipers (except for the somewhat esoteric types like this writer who have at their disposal the luxury of a theological education and the oddity of a fascination with the thoughts of the church Fathers), it does considerable violence to the role of the Hebrew scriptures in our lectionary. The Hebrew Testament story becomes a mere scaffold or backdrop to that of the Christian Testament. There are more profound reasons than that for reading the Christian scriptures in the light of the Hebrew, as there are more profound reasons than that for the identification of the Christian Easter as the Christian celebration of the passover.

The liturgy does use the Hebrew scriptures as a Christian book. This is clearly enunciated as a principle in No. 5 of the Introduction: "The New Testament lies hidden in the Old; the Old Testament comes fully to light in the New. Christ himself is the center and fullness of all of Scripture, as he is of the entire liturgy." The principle is carried out in a thoroughgoing way in the arrangement of the lectionary and in the ceremonial directives for the reading of the scriptures in the assembly. The gospel appears in every way as the primary reading, a principle put into practice in a thoroughgoing way insofar as there is no Sunday sequential reading of any of the Hebrew scriptures. Instead, the Hebrew scripture reading is always chosen because of its relation to the gospel of the day. The same is true of the responsorial psalm.

This usage is, of course, traditional. It is, indeed, axiomatic for the writers of the New Testament, who freely reinterpret the Hebrew scriptures in the light of the Christian experience. It means, however, that the liturgy appears to use the Hebrew scriptures as not having value in their own right, independent of the Christian experience. We may regret the failure of ecumenical good manners. The Hebrew scriptures have not ceased to be the word of God for the Jews, and they are the word of God for them independent of any relation to Christ. We might have expected at least the acknowledgement of a variant use of sacred scripture in a sister tradition.[8]

---

[8]In the cycle of "ordinary time," the use of Hebrew scriptures non-sequentially so that they coincide with gospel stories taking up the same themes does indeed

At the same time, something needs to be said about the legitimacy of using the Hebrew scriptures the way we do. To say that it is "traditional" is not to say that it is legitimate, but only that we have always done it this way. In what way, then, can we say that this traditional usage is legitimate (which is not to say that such a usage is the *only* possible way of interpreting the Hebrew scriptures)?

My own suggestion is that the Christian liturgical use of the Hebrew scripture texts must be understood in the light of the particular relation between the church and the scripture that is presupposed in our liturgical structures. That is to say, the presupposition is that a Christian assembly is itself a real sacramental presence of Christ. It is Christ present in the Spirit in the midst of God's people that gives the Christian assembly its special identity. It understands itself as called together by God to be a presence of Christ in the Spirit, an understanding that is enshrined in the very greetings between priest and people that begin our assemblies. Anything the assembly does, with and through its ministers, whether in proclamation of word or celebration of sacrament, is thus a sacramental action of Christ in the world. Granted that this is in every way a mystery, obscured by the darkness of human sin and ineptness, that presence of Christ is still understood to be real and actual. Within the context of a Christian assembly, then, the proclamation of the word inevitably has a Christian aura. The scriptures will be read against the horizon of the fundamental experience of Christ present in the midst of the assembly. This is why the Introduction appeals to the story of Christ in the synagogue at Nazareth (No. 3) and to the story of the disciples on the road to Emmaus (No. 10). Christ is seen "in" the Hebrew scripture text, not because Christians have some sort of key to a "deeper and fuller sense" hidden like the kernel in a husk, but because their experience of Christ coincides in some significant way with the experience of God in Israel. The God whom we worship in our liturgy is not, first of all, the God of the Book (which is why we freely interpret the Book by arranging it in a lectionary). Our God is the God of the Gathering. The sacred texts are used to probe the meaning of that presence of the God of the Gathering. In using the scriptures, the church is saying to itself, "Where do we find

---

tend to foster the old impression that the Hebrew Scriptures are a mere scaffold or backdrop to the new. Happily, the ecumenical Consultation on Common Texts (we share essentially the same lectionary now with a number of North American Churches—Episcopalians, Lutherans, Presbyterians, and United Methodists) has prepared a revision that corrects this fault, and that revision has been approved for experimental use by the Roman Catholic Bishops in the United States.

evidence that will help us name the God present in our midst, and trace the shape of God's paths among us?" In a Christian gathering, grounded in God's presence through Christ in the Spirit, the scriptures will inevitably be used to trace more fully the shape of that specifically Christian experience. Since Vatican II, official documents describe the presence of Christ under the forms of bread and wine by the technical term "substantial." They choose the term "substantial" because Christ's presence under the forms of bread and wine is only *one* mode of sacramental presence. Christ is sacramentally present in the assembly, in its ministers, in the proclamation of the word, and in the actions of all the other sacraments.

It is these principles that underlie the assertion of No. 68 that "an organic harmony of themes designed to aid homiletic instruction" would "conflict with the genuine conception of liturgical celebration." As the Introduction goes on to say, "The liturgy is always the celebration of the mystery of Christ and makes use of the word of God on the basis of its own tradition, guided not by merely logical or intrinsic concerns but by the desire to proclaim the Gospel and to lead those who believe to the fullness of truth." In other words, the liturgy is not *about* some idea or other (however worthy of consideration or however true), but *is* the mystery of Christ present among us. The "fullness of truth" is not a set of ideas or facts, but God enfleshed among us. This does not mean, of course, that the proclamation of the word avoids the "issues of real life," but that those issues are to be held up against the light of that life present and shared among us. This, I must insist again, only makes sense if people perceive themselves as a people consecrated by baptism and confirmation to be that presence in the world. Conventional preaching and thematic celebration assume that people are in fact baptized catechumens, still learning what the Christian message is about. Worse, they are often simply accommodations to a failure to give primary attention to the building of a community where a diversity of ministries and gifts are shared. If people do not have a sense of shared mission, the better part of the Christian message cannot be heard. Real sacramental celebration assumes that there is something (or rather some One) to celebrate, and that a significant core of those present know it.

The point, then, of celebrating the Easter vigil as our night of passover, and of giving so much attention to the story of the crossing of the Red Sea, is that we celebrate our own reality as people on a journey. Israel did not tell and retell the story of the crossing because it experienced its history as a moving from glory to glory:

quite the contrary. The story itself is only the summation of a larger story of struggle, and the larger story includes the story of Israel's enslavement in Egypt, its reluctance to follow Moses, its trial, wandering, and hesitation in the desert, and its struggle to enter the promised land. That story of the Exodus has been told and retold in places of exile and in spaces of defeat more often than it has been celebrated in Jerusalem. The point of the story is not that God is a magician who rescues his people in Cecil B. DeMille spectaculars, but that in a history fraught with defeat and failure and exile, Israel discovered itself to be in covenant with God, a people blessed and graced, not somewhere apart from its trials, but in the midst of them.

Likewise, in naming ourselves as a people identified with Christ in the Spirit through baptism, we are not saying that we emerge from the font never to sin again, but simply that our God dwells in the midst of this struggling people. The point of telling the stories of Christ's temptation and transfiguration at the beginning of Lent, and the story of the way to the cross at the end, is not to set Christ up as an impossible example. Rather, these Christian versions of the Exodus story (the temptation portrays Jesus as undergoing the trials of Israel in the desert, as the transfiguration is in many ways an account that parallels the coming of the glory of God upon Israel in the covenant at Sinai) are read so that we can see, in our own struggles, Christ's identification with us. The invitation is to find the hidden glory of God in the midst of our own history. This is why the Holy Week liturgies have a somewhat paradoxical character: the joyous hosannas of the Palm Sunday procession juxtaposed with the reading of the passion, the festivity of Holy Thursday in the midst of the foreboding before the story of Christ's impending death, the use of festal red vestments on Good Friday. The point is that the presence of Christ is not somehow separable from our ordinary lives of trial and struggle. We would be considerably more alert to this if in the reading of the passion the ministers took the part of the crowd and the congregation took the part of Christ. As was mentioned earlier, it is only the leaflet missals (and not the official liturgical books) that encourage the opposite.

During the Easter Season, readings from the Acts of the Apostles are substituted for the usual Hebrew Scripture readings. This exactly parallels the summation of Israel's history, which runs through Lent and into the Easter vigil. For the Easter season is a celebration of the work of the Spirit in the church (Pentecost means "fiftieth day," and it refers to the "pentecostal" fifty days after Easter). Here again, as in the Easter season gospels, the struggles of the early church come to the fore. The resurrection stories are stories of loss as well as of gain—full of doubting and dismayed disciples, and of the nostalgia for the days of the Lord's "earthly" (i.e., historic) ministry. To proclaim the resurrection is also to proclaim the absence of Jesus as he was in the days of that ministry. Likewise, the story of the work of the Spirit in Acts is a story of a Spirit who must continually overcome the church's conservatism and recalcitrance, its blindness, stubborness, and squabbling, its differences of ethnicity, and its varieties of interpretation of the Christian message. The Book of Acts opens with Jesus' departure, the suicide of one of the Twelve, and the disciples casting lots to fill the gap; it ends with St. Paul imprisoned with the shadow of the Roman axe over his head. In the middle it turns on a dispute over the interpretation of divine law. Yet it celebrates the work of the Spirit in the midst of that history. The season *closes* with Pentecost, a celebration that comes at the end of the narration of the trials of the disciples and the early church. It comes as an affirmation that the Spirit moves on as much in spite of the church as because of it, moves on in the midst of the seaminess of its everyday, every-year, every-century life.

The paschal season (Lent through Pentecost) is normally the time for the celebration of initiation for new adult Christians. It begins with their election on the first Sunday of Lent, moves on to the "scrutinies" on the third, fourth, and fifth Sundays,[9] culminates in their being baptized, confirmed, and fully participating for the first time in the eucharist at the Easter vigil, and concludes with the period of "mystagogy" during the Easter season—actually a kind of "debriefing," a beginning of coming to grips with the fact that while they may have found home, enlightenment, and new life, holy mother church is not exactly a fairy princess.

The point of this public celebration is less to "do something" to or for the candidates, than for them to "do something" for the assembly of the church. As new and fresh witnesses to the faith, these new adult Christins are the living proclamation of the resurrection. Their journey into faith is a witness to the life that is among us. Their fast from the eucharist during Lent, when they are dismissed from the assembly at the end of the liturgy of the word, is less for their benefit than for ours—so that we can savor the

---

[9]The actual purpose of these "scrutinies" is to prayerfully celebrate the identification of these people with the gospel story, as people who were once outsiders now coming home, as blind and now seeing from a new perspective, as finding new life.

weight of what we are doing. On the days of election and scrutiny, their story should be made accessible to the assembly, so that there is a real point to publicly celebrating the sacraments of their initiation on Easter eve. They should also have public visibility during the Easter season, so that they can continue their role as new witnesses to the life among us. The insertion of anonymous candidates into the Easter vigil without the Lenten preliminary elections and scrutinies, and without the Easter "mystagogy" celebrated publicly, simply encourages the same magical view of sacraments we have entertained for centuries.

If Lent is about "following Christ," then it is about the effort to trace the marks of Christ's journey in our own lives. If Easter is about "the resurrection," then it is about discerning the life in the Spirit as it is lived in a struggling community of far less than perfect disciples. And if Pentecost is about the "coming of the Spirit," then it is about ourselves as a community of faith that must be ever-alert to the possibility of surprise and change.

Christmas is the church's celebration of divine judgment. The morbid preoccupation with divine judgment as nothing but wrath and woe, which has so inflamed the Christian imagination (though rarely inflamed it to moral improvement, much less social conscience), makes this notion difficult to swallow. But the point of the story of the child at Bethlehem, unfolding into the adoration of the magi with their royal gifts, and finding its summation in the aged Jewish Simeon's rejoicing over the coming of the light to the nations, and the point of all the language of royalty—identification of Jesus with the royal house of David, the conflict with Herod, and all the rest—is that God's ways are not our ways. The festival is centered on the lowly birth at Bethlehem, not for us to wax sentimental about the lovely baby, but to drive home the point that God's rule is in no way like the exertion of any human power. The point of Advent is not to "prepare for the birth of Jesus" (that happened far away and long ago), but to sharpen our perception of what the reign of God looks like when it overtakes us. It does not look like power and glory as we know them.

In the lectionary, there is a significant "pre-Advent"; the November gospels call attention to the imminent judgment of God. There is also a kind of "pre-Christmas" in the festival of Christ the King, and it is integrally related to those judgment gospels. The divine judgment is not the judgment of a despot, of an angry parent, or of a celestial bookkeeper, but the judgment of a God who embraces the world in love. That last Sunday of the old year is at the same time a bridge to the new: at the center of God's judgment is a concern for the poor, the lowly, and the outcast. The feast of Christ the King's call to build the world in justice and peace focuses the implications of divine judgment. The fiery figure of John the Baptist, who occupies the center of the stage in the Advent gospels with his call to repentance, has already, in the ending of the preceding year, had his warnings underscored by the preaching of Jesus himself. The point is that our God is relentlessly serious, and that the coming of God has everything to do with holiness, righteousness, and justice in the world.

Yet all of this is set against the prophecies of Isaiah, not simply as "background," but as lending substance to the gospel view of divine judgment. The Isaian prophecies spoke for the hope of a defeated nation, and defeated indeed because in the eyes of the prophet it had failed to do justice and to love mercy. There is both warning and tenderness in the Christmas cycle—because the God of Scripture identifies with the poor, the lowly, and the outcast. This is at the same time affliction for the comfortable and comfort for the afflicted.

Christmas itself is "framed" by stories about Mary, and any serious effort at contemporary Marian devotion would look here, especially to the last Sunday of Advent, to the Bethlehem stories, and to the Solemnity of Mary (New Year's Day), as its primary source. She appears as the prototype of all faithful believers. We refer not to the simpering submissiveness plastered on her by debased devotion, but to the scriptural portrayal of her as one who struggles with what it means to believe, and who strives to live in joyous hope despite the ambiguities and uncertainties and deprivations of her situation.

The somewhat "tough" tone of pre-Advent and the first Sundays of Advent gives way to the joy of the Christmas festival itself, unfolding into the celebration of the twin Sundays of the Epiphany and the Baptism of the Lord; their point being that as baptized Gentiles, we too are heirs of the promise to Israel. The point, however, in the adoration of the magi and Jesus' baptism at the hands of the wild desert prophet, is still that the coming of the reign of God is to be found in unlikely and unexpected places, and that it is utterly contrary to the expectations of the conventionally pious, the impressively righteous, or the obviously powerful. There is plenty here to call us as a community of sinners identified with the risen Lord in the Spirit.